42

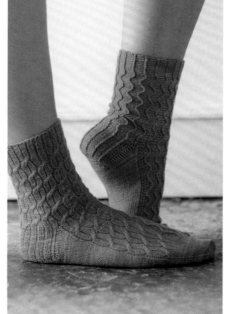

18

6

54

Contents

CoopKnits

CREDITS
Publisher & Author: Rachel Coopey
Technical Editor: Jen Arnall-Culliford
Art & Production Editor: Nic Blackmore
Photography: Jesse Wild
Pattern Checking: Susan Crawford
Models: Caroline White
Jeni Hewlett
Jen Arnall-Culliford

Yarns used: Blue Moon Fiber Arts
Fyberspates
The Knitting Goddess
Madelinetosh
Malabrigo
Opal
Socktopus

COOPKNITS SOCKS
First published in 2013 by Rachel Coopey
© Copyright Rachel Coopey 2013
All rights reserved
All images in this publication © Jesse Wild 2013

Printed by Williams Press, Berkshire, UK

British Library Cataloguing in Publication Data:
A catalogue record for this book is available from
the British Library. ISBN-978-0-9576216-0-2

CoopKnits

Socks

VOLUME 1

RACHEL COOPEY

12

48

36

60

30

24

Introduction

I was taught to knit by my grandmother and mother when I was little and I still have the extremely long garter stitch scarf to prove it!

When I rediscovered knitting in 2007, I wanted to learn everything. I roped in my mother, and anyone else I could find, to teach me all the techniques they knew.

I was drawn to sock knitting when I bought 3 skeins of hand-dyed sock yarn – they were so beautiful I thought I'd give knitting a pair of socks a try. When I turned the heel on that first sock, I felt like I'd performed a magic trick! I pulled it out of my knitting bag and showed it to everyone I met, shouting 'Look! Look what I made! It's a SOCK!' (I got varying degrees of enthusiasm in return, but I think it's fair to say no-one was *quite* as excited as me).

I haven't stopped knitting socks since then and I designed my first pair in 2010, I love the portability of socks, the intricacy and the usefulness of the finished object – there really is nothing like hand-knitted socks for warming your heart and your feet.

Rachel x

Bold lines of cables and twisted stitches on these bright socks were inspired by the shapes and colours of marker buoys bobbing on the water.

Dawlish

Dawlish

YARN
Fyberspates Vivacious 4ply (100% superwash merino; 365m per 100g skein)
Sunshine (604), 1 x 100g skein

NEEDLES
2.25mm [UK 13/US 1] 80cm [30in] circular needles or DPNs (or size needed to get gauge)
Cable needle
Tapestry needle
Stitch markers

TENSION
36 sts and 50 rows = 10cm [4in] over st st
46 sts and 52 rows = 10cm [4in] over unstretched cable patterns

SIZES
Small (Large)
To fit foot circumference: 20 (25.5) cm [8 (10) in]
Actual foot circumference of sock, unstretched:
17 (19) cm [6.75 (7.5) in]

ABBREVIATIONS
2/1 RC: Slip next st to cable needle and place at back of work, k2, then k1 from cable needle
2/1 LC: Slip next 2 sts to cable needle and place at front of work, k1, then k2 from cable needle
1/1 LPC: Slip next st to cable needle and place at front of work, p1, then k1 from cable needle
1/1 RPC: Slip next st to cable needle and place at back of work, k1, then p1 from cable needle

See full list of abbreviations on page 66.

PATTERN NOTES
There are different charts for each sock, as the cables mirror each other.
Written instructions for the chart patterns are given on the following page.

SOCK ONE

CUFF

Cast on 68 (76) sts. Distribute sts over your needles as desired and join to work in the round, being careful not to twist. Place marker for start of round.

Round 1: *Reading from right to left, work from row 1 of chart A, repeating the marked section 1 (2) times in total; repeat from * once more. Repeat last round 19 more times to create rib pattern.

Round 21: *Reading from right to left, work from row 2 of chart A, repeating the marked section 1 (2) times in total; repeat from * once more.

LEG

Round 1: *P1, work row 1 of chart B over next 15 sts, p2, k0 (2), p0 (2), work row 1 of chart C over next 15 sts, p1; repeat from * once more.

Round 2: *P1, work row 2 of chart B over next 15 sts, p2, k0 (2), p0 (2), work row 2 of chart C over next 15 sts, p1; repeat from * once more.

Last 2 rounds set charts B and C patterns, with purl (and knit in large size only) columns between charts. Continue to work as set until chart row 40 is completed. Then work rows 1-18 once more.

HEEL SET-UP

Next round (heel set-up): P1, work row 19 of chart B over next 15 sts, p2, k0 (2), p0 (2), work row 19 of chart C over next 15 sts, p2, work row 19 of chart B over next 15 sts, p2, k0 (2), p0 (2), work row 19 of chart C over next 15 sts. Leave remaining st unworked.

HEEL FLAP

Turn work so WS is facing. Heel flap will be worked back and forth on the next 32 (36) sts, beginning with a WS row. keep remaining 36 (40) sts on needles for instep.

Row 1 (WS): Sl1 wyif, p1, k3, p2, k1, p2, k3, [p2, k2] 1 (2) times, p2, k3, p2, k1, p2, k3, p2.

Row 2 (RS): Sl1 wyib, k1, p3, k2, p1, k2, p3, [k2, p2] 1 (2) times, k2, p3, k2, p1, k2, p3, k2.

Repeat these 2 rows 14 more times then work row 1 once more.

TURN HEEL

Row 1 (RS): Sl1 wyib, k18 (20), ssk, k1, turn, leaving remaining 10 (12) sts unworked.

Row 2: Sl1 wyif, p7, p2tog, p1, turn, leaving remaining 10 (12) sts unworked.

Row 3: Sl1 wyib, k to 1 st before gap, ssk, k1, turn.

Row 4: Sl1 wyif, p to 1 st before gap, p2tog, p1, turn.

Repeat last 2 rows 4 (5) more times. All sts have been worked. 20 (22) heel sts remain.

GUSSET

Set-up Round: Sl1, k19 (21), pick up and knit 16 sts along edge of heel flap (1 stitch in each slipped stitch along the edge of the flap), work across instep sts as foll: P2tog, work row 20 of chart B over next 15 sts, p2, k0 (2), p0 (2), work row 20 of chart C over next 15 sts, p2tog, pick up and knit 16 sts along edge of heel flap, k36 (38). place marker for new start of round (at start of instep stitches). 86 (92) sts.

Round 1: P1, work row 21 of chart B, p2, k0 (2), p0 (2), work row 21 of chart C, p1, ssk, k to 2 sts before end of round, k2tog. 84 (90) sts.

Round 2: P1, work row 22 of chart B, p2, k0 (2), p0 (2), work row 22 of chart C, p1, k to end of round.

Last 2 rounds set chart patterns and gusset decreases. Repeat these 2 rounds 8 (7) more times, working next row of charts each time. 68 (76) sts.

You should now have 34 (38) sts each on instep and sole.

FOOT

Work as set (with charts and purl (and knit in large size only) columns on instep sts and st st on the sole) until the sock measures 5cm [2in] less than the desired foot length.

TOE

Round 1: Knit.

Round 2: K1, ssk, k28 (32), k2tog, k1, pm, k1, ssk, k28 (32), k2tog, k1. 64 (72) sts.

Round 3: Knit.

Round 4: *K1, ssk, k to 3 sts before marker, k2tog, k1, slm; repeat from * once more. 60 (68) sts.

Repeat last 2 rounds 10 (11) more times. 20 (24) sts.

Cut yarn, leaving a 30cm [12in] tail. Graft sts together using kitchener stitch. Weave in ends.

SOCK TWO

CUFF

Work as Sock One, using chart D instead of chart A.

LEG

Round 1: *P1, work row 1 of chart C over next 15 sts, p2, k0 (2), p0 (2), work row 1 of chart B over next 15 sts, p1; repeat from * once more.

Round 2: *P1, work row 2 of chart C over next 15 sts, p2, k0 (2), p0 (2), work row 2 of chart B over next 15 sts, p1; repeat from * once more.

Last 2 rounds set charts C and B patterns (order is reversed from Sock One), with purl (and knit in large size only) columns between charts. Continue to work as set until chart row 40 is completed. Then work rows 1-18 once more.

HEEL SET-UP

Next round (heel set-up): P1, work row 19 of chart C over next 15 sts, p2, k0 (2), p0 (2), work row 19 of chart B over next 15 sts, p2, work row 19 of chart C over next 15 sts, p2, k0 (2), p0 (2), work row 19 of chart B over next 15 sts.

Leave remaining st unworked.

HEEL FLAP AND HEEL TURN

Work as for Sock One.

GUSSET

Work as for Sock One, but keeping charts B and C as established (order reversed from Sock One).

FOOT AND TOE

Work as for Sock One.

Charts

CHART C: CABLE

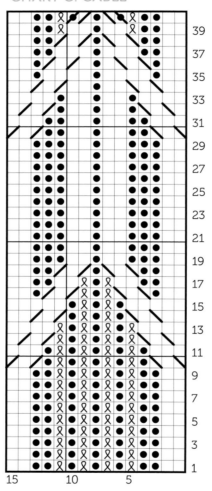

CHART B: CABLE

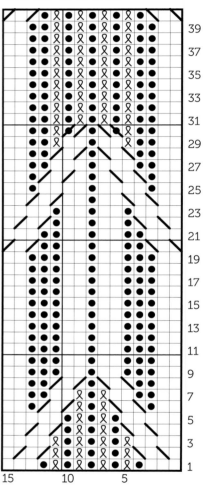

KEY

☐	Knit
●	Purl
⏽	K1 tbl
◯	Yarnover
⧄ ⧄	2/1 RC
⧅ ⧅	2/1 LC
⧅	1/1 LPC
⧄	1/1 RPC
☐	Pattern repeat

CHART D: SOCK TWO CUFF

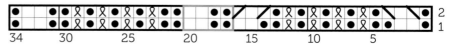

CHART A: SOCK ONE CUFF

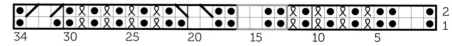

WRITTEN CHART INSTRUCTIONS

CHART A: SOCK ONE CUFF

Row 1: P1, k2, p2, [k1 tbl, p1] 4 times, p1, k2, [p2, k2] 1 (2) times, p2, [k1 tbl, p1] 4 times, p1, k2, p1.

Row 2: P1, 2/1 LC, [p1, k1 tbl] 4 times, p1, 2/1 RC, [p2, k2] 1 (2) times, p2, [k1 tbl, p1] 4 times, p1, k2, p1.

CHART B: CABLE

Row 1: K3, [p1, k1 tbl] 4 times, p1, k3.

Row 2: K1, 2/1 LC, [k1 tbl, p1] 3 times, k1 tbl, 2/1 RC, k1.

Row 3: K4, [k1 tbl, p1] 3 times, k1 tbl, k4.

Row 4: K2, 2/1 LC, [p1, k1 tbl] 2 times, p1, 2/1 RC, k2.

Row 5: K5, [p1, k1 tbl] 2 times, p1, k5.

Row 6: K2, p1, 2/1 LC, k1 tbl, p1, k1 tbl, 2/1 RC, p1, k2.

Row 7: K2, p2, k2, k1 tbl, p1, k1 tbl, k2, p2, k2.

Row 8: K2, p2, 2/1 LC, p1, 2/1 RC, p2, k2.

Rows 9-19: K2, p3, k2, p1, k2, p3, k2.

Row 20: 2/1 LC, p2, k2, p1, k2, p2, 2/1 RC.

Row 21: K3, p2, k2, p1, k2, p2, k3.

Row 22: K1, 2/1 LC, p1, k2, p1, k2, p1, 2/1 RC, k1.

Row 23: K4, [p1, k2] 2 times, p1, k4.

Row 24: K2, 2/1 LC, k2, p1, k2, 2/1 RC, k2.

Row 25: K2, p1, k4, p1, k4, p1, k2.

Row 26: K2, p1, 2/1 LC, k1, p1, k1, 2/1 RC, p1, k2.

Row 27: K2, p2, k3, p1, k3, p2, k2.

Row 28: K2, p2, 2/1 LC, p1, 2/1 RC, p2, k2.

Row 29: K2, p2, k1 tbl, k2, p1, k2, k1 tbl, p2, k2.

Row 30: K2, p2, k1 tbl, 1/1 LpC, p1, 1/1 RpC, k1 tbl, p2, k2.

Rows 31-39: K2, p2, [k1 tbl, p1] 4 times, p1, k2.

Row 40: 2/1 LC, [p1, k1 tbl] 4 times, p1, 2/1 RC.

CHART C: CABLE

Rows 1-9: K2, p2, [k1 tbl, p1] 4 times, p1, k2.

Row 10: 2/1 LC, [p1, k1 tbl] 4 times, p1, 2/1 RC.

Row 11: K3, [p1, k1 tbl] 4 times, p1, k3.

Row 12: K1, 2/1 LC, [k1 tbl, p1] 3 times, k1 tbl, 2/1 RC, k1.

Row 13: K4, [k1 tbl, p1] 3 times, k1 tbl, k4.

Row 14: K2, 2/1 LC, [p1, k1 tbl] 2 times, p1, 2/1 RC, k2.

Row 15: K5, [p1, k1 tbl] 2 times, p1, k5.

Row 16: K2, p1, 2/1 LC, k1 tbl, p1, k1 tbl, 2/1 RC, p1, k2.

Row 17: K2, p2, k2, k1 tbl, p1, k1 tbl, k2, p2, k2.

Row 18: K2, p2, 2/1 LC, p1, 2/1 RC, p2, k2.

Rows 19-29: K2, p3, k2, p1, k2, p3, k2.

Row 30: 2/1 LC, p2, k2, p1, k2, p2, 2/1 RC.

Row 31: K3, p2, k2, p1, k2, p2, k3.

Row 32: K1, 2/1 LC, p1, k2, p1, k2, p1, 2/1 RC, k1.

Row 33: K4, [p1, k2] 2 times, p1, k4.

Row 34: K2, 2/1 LC, k2, p1, k2, 2/1 RC, k2.

Row 35: K2, p1, k4, p1, k4, p1, k2.

Row 36: K2, p1, 2/1 LC, k1, p1, k1, 2/1 RC, p1, k2.

Row 37: K2, p2, k3, p1, k3, p2, k2.

Row 38: K2, p2, 2/1 LC, p1, 2/1 RC, p2, k2.

Row 39: K2, p2, k1 tbl, k2, p1, k2, k1 tbl, p2, k2.

Row 40: K2, p2, k1 tbl, 1/1 LpC, p1, 1/1 RpC, k1 tbl, p2, k2.

CHART D: SOCK TWO CUFF

Row 1: P1, k2, p2, [k1 tbl, p1] 3 times, k1 tbl, [p2, k2] 1 (2) times, p2, k2, p2, [k1 tbl, p1] 4 times, p1, k2, p1.

Row 2: P1, k2, p2, [k1 tbl, p1] 3 times, k1 tbl, [p2, k2] 1 (2) times, p2, 2/1 LC, [p1, k1 tbl] 4 times, p1, 2/1 RC, p1.

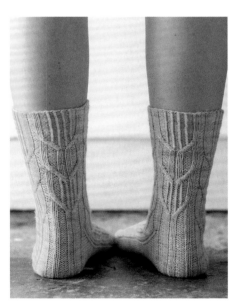
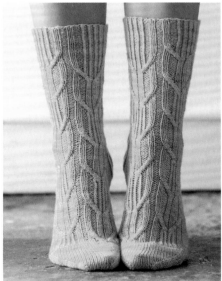
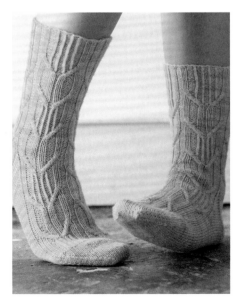

Milfoil

Leafy lace and wrapped stitch patterns entwine these socks. Designed to be odd, the leg and foot of each sock are opposites.

Milfoil

YARN
Malabrigo Sock (100% superwash merino;
403m per 100g skein)
Lettuce (37), 1 x 100g skein

NEEDLES
2.25mm [UK 13/US 1] 80cm [30in] circular needles
or DPNs (or size needed to get gauge)
Cable needle
Tapestry needle
Stitch markers

TENSION
36 sts and 50 rows = 10cm [4in] over st st
35.5 sts and 48 rows = 10cm [4in] over unstretched
lace patterns

SIZES
Small (Large)
To fit foot circumference: 20 (25.5) cm [8 (10) in]
Actual foot circumference of sock, unstretched: 18
(21) cm [7 (8.25) in]

ABBREVIATIONS
Wrap 3: K3 onto cable needle, wrap yarn twice
around these stitches by bringing yarn to front of
work between the left needle and the cable needle
and wrapping yarn to back of work between cable
needle and right needle, then slip the 3 stitches
from the cable needle to the right needle.

See full list of abbreviations on page 66.

PATTERN NOTES
These socks are designed to be complementary,
rather than identical. If you prefer identical socks,
make 2 of Sock One or 2 of Sock Two.
Written instructions for the charts appear on the
following page.

SOCK ONE

CUFF

Cast on 64 (72) sts. Distribute sts over your needles as desired and join to work in the round, being careful not to twist. Place marker for start of round.

Small size only
Round 1: *K1 tbl, p1; repeat from * to end.

Large size only
Round 1: *[K1 tbl, p1] 3 times, k1 tbl, p2; repeat from * to end.

Both sizes
Last round sets rib pattern. Work this round 15 more times.

LEG

Round 1: Reading from right to left, work from row 1 of chart A (B), repeating the 8 (9)-stitch motif 4 times in total, work from row 1 of chart C (D), repeating the 8 (9)-stitch motif 4 times in total.
Last round sets charts A (B) and C (D) patterns. Continue to work from charts as set until 59 rows have been worked in pattern in total (chart A (B) has been completed 4 times, then rows 1-11 have been worked once more).

HEEL SET-UP

Next round: Reading from right to left, work from row 12 of chart A (B), repeating the 8 (9)-stitch motif 4 times in total, work from row 4 of chart C (D), repeating the 8 (9)-stitch motif 3 times in total, work a further 7 sts from row 4 of chart C (D), thus leaving 1 (2) sts unworked at the end of the round.

HEEL FLAP

Turn work so WS is facing. Heel flap will be worked back and forth on the next 31 (34) sts, beginning with a WS row. Keep remaining 33 (38) sts on needles for instep.

Small size only
Row 1 (WS): Sl1 wyif, p30.
Row 2 (RS): *Sl1 wyib, k1; repeat from * until 1 st remains, k1.

Large size only
Row 1 (WS): Sl1 wyif, p33.
Row 2 (RS): *[Sl1 wyib, k1] 3 times, sl1 wyib, k2; repeat from * 2 more times, [sl1 wyib, k1] 3 times, k1.

Both sizes
Repeat last 2 rows 14 more times then work row 1 once more.

TURN HEEL

Row 1 (RS): Sl1 wyib, k17 (18), ssk, k1, turn, leaving remaining 10 (12) sts unworked.
Row 2: Sl1 wyif, p6 (5), p2tog, p1, turn, leaving remaining 10 (12) sts unworked.
Row 3: Sl1 wyib, k to 1 st before gap, ssk, k1, turn.
Row 4: Sl1 wyif, p to 1 st before gap, p2tog, p1, turn.
Repeat last 2 rows 4 (5) more times. All heel sts have been worked. 19 (20) heel sts remain.

GUSSET

Set-up Round: Sl1, k18 (19), pick up and knit 16 sts along edge of heel flap (1 stitch in each slipped stitch along the edge of the flap), work across instep sts as foll: P1 (2), work from row 1 of chart C (D) 4 times across instep sts, pick up and knit 16 sts along edge of heel flap, k35 (36). Place marker for new start of round (at start of instep stitches). 84 (90) sts.
Round 1: P1 (2), work from row 2 of chart C (D), repeating 8 (9)-stitch motif 4 times, ssk, k to 2 sts before end of round, k2tog. 82 (88) sts.
Round 2: P1 (2), work from row 3 of chart C (D), repeating 8 (9)-stitch motif 4 times, k to end of round.

Pattern continues on page 17.

Milfoil

Charts

CHART D: LARGE

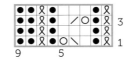

CHART C: SMALL

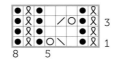

CHART B: LARGE

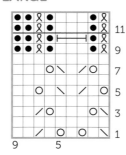

CHART A: SMALL

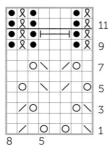

KEY

☐	Knit
●	Purl
⋉	K1 tbl
╲	SSK
╱	K2tog
○	Yarnover
⊢—⊣	Wrap 3
☐	Pattern repeat

WRITTEN CHART INSTRUCTIONS

CHART A: SMALL
Row 1: Ssk, k1, yo, k1, yo, k1, k2tog, k1.
Rows 2, 4, 6 and 8: K8.
Row 3: Ssk, yo, k3, yo, k2tog, k1.
Row 5: Yo, k1, k2tog, k1, ssk, k1, yo, k1.
Row 7: K1, yo, k2tog, k1, ssk, yo, k2.
Row 9: K1 tbl, p1, k3, p1, k1 tbl, p1.
Row 10: K1 tbl, p1, wrap 3, p1, k1 tbl, p1.
Rows 11 and 12: As row 9.

CHART B: LARGE
Row 1: Ssk, k1, yo, k1, yo, k1, k2tog, k2.
Rows 2, 4, 6 and 8: K9.
Row 3: Ssk, yo, k3, yo, k2tog, k2.
Row 5: Yo, k1, k2tog, k1, ssk, k1, yo, k2.
Row 7: K1, yo, k2tog, k1, ssk, yo, k3.
Row 9: K1 tbl, p1, k3, p1, k1 tbl, p2.
Row 10: K1 tbl, p1, wrap 3, p1, k1 tbl, p2.
Rows 11 and 12: As row 9.

CHART C: SMALL
Row 1: K1 tbl, p1, k1, ssk, yo, p1, k1 tbl, p1.
Row 2: K1 tbl, p1, k3, p1, k1 tbl, p1.
Row 3: K1 tbl, p1, yo, k2tog, k1, p1, k1 tbl, p1.
Row 4: As row 2.

CHART D: LARGE
Row 1: K1 tbl, p1, k1, ssk, yo, p1, k1 tbl, p2.
Row 2: K1 tbl, p1, k3, p1, k1 tbl, p2.
Row 3: K1 tbl, p1, yo, k2tog, k1, p1,
k1 tbl, p2.
Row 4: As row 2.

Last 2 rounds set chart C (D) pattern on instep, and gusset decreases. Repeat these 2 rounds 9 (7) more times, working next row of chart each time. 64 (74) sts.
You should now have 33 (38) sts on the instep and 31 (36) sts on the sole.

FOOT

Work as set (chart C (D) on instep and st st on sole) without further shaping until sock measures 5cm [2in] less than the desired foot length.

TOE

Round 1: K1, ssk, k27 (32), k2tog, k1, pm, knit to end. 62 (72) sts.
Round 2: Knit.
Round 3: *K1, ssk, k to 3 sts before marker, k2tog, k1, slm; repeat from * once more. 58 (68) sts.
Repeat last 2 rounds 10 (11) more times. 18 (24) sts.
Cut yarn, leaving a 30cm [12in] tail.
Graft sts together using Kitchener stitch.
Weave in ends.

SOCK TWO

CUFF
Work as Sock One.

LEG
Round 1: Reading from right to left, work from row 1 of chart C (D), repeating the 8 (9)-stitch motif 4 times in total, work from row 1 of chart A (B), repeating the 8 (9)-stitch motif 4 times in total.
Last round sets charts C (D) and A (B) patterns (order reversed from Sock One). Continue to work from charts as set until 59 rows have been worked in pattern in total (chart A (B) has been completed 4 times, then rows 1-11 have been worked once more).

HEEL SET-UP
Next round: Reading from right to left, work from row 4 of chart C (D), repeating the 8 (9)-stitch motif 4 times in total, work from row 12 of chart A (B), repeating the 8 (9)-stitch motif 3 times in total, work a

further 7 sts from row 12 of chart A (B), thus leaving 1 (2) sts unworked at the end of the round.

HEEL FLAP AND HEEL TURN
Work as Sock One.

GUSSET
Set-up Round: Sl1, k18 (19), pick up and knit 16 sts along edge of heel flap (1 stitch in each slipped stitch along the edge of the flap), work across instep sts as foll: P1 (2), work from row 1 of chart A (B) 4 times across instep sts, pick up and knit 16 sts along edge of heel flap, k35 (36). Place marker for new start of round (at start of instep stitches). 84 (90) sts.

Round 1: P1 (2), work from row 2 of chart A (B), repeating 8 (9)-stitch motif 4 times, ssk, k to 2 sts before end of round, k2tog. 82 (88) sts.
Round 2: P1 (2), work from row 3 of chart A (B), repeating 8 (9)-stitch motif 4 times, k to end of round.
Last 2 rounds set chart A (B) pattern on instep, and gusset decreases. Repeat these 2 rounds 9 (7) more times, working next row of chart each time. 64 (74) sts.
You should now have 33 (38) sts on the instep and 31 (36) sts on the sole.

FOOT AND TOE
Work as for Sock One to end, using chart A (B) instead of chart C (D) on the instep sts.

Budleigh

Rippling cables and twisted stitches flow along these socks, inspired by the sandy ridges left by an outgoing tide.

Budleigh

YARN
The Knitting Goddess Merino and Nylon Sock (75% merino, 25% nylon; 212m per 50g skein)
Semi-solid Turquoise, 2 x 50g skeins

NEEDLES
2.25mm [UK 13/US 1] 80cm [30in] circular needles or DPNs (or size needed to get gauge)
Cable needle
Tapestry needle
Stitch markers

TENSION
36 sts and 50 rows = 10cm [4in] over st st
28 sts = 7.5cm [2.75in] over single twisted stitch pattern
35 sts = 8cm [3in] over unstretched cable pattern

SIZES
Small (Medium, Large)
To fit foot circumference: 20 (23, 25.5) cm [8 (9, 10) in]
Actual foot circumference of sock (cables unstretched): 17 (19.5, 21.5) cm [6.75 (7.75, 8.5) in]

ABBREVIATIONS
2/1/2 RPC: Slip next 3 sts to cable needle and place at back of work, k2, slip left-most st from cable needle back on to LH needle, move cable needle with remaining sts to front of work, p1 from LH needle, then k2 from cable needle.
2/1/2 LPC: Slip next 3 sts to cable needle and place at front of work, k2, move left-most st from cable needle back on to LH needle, p this st, then k2 from cable needle.
1/1 LPT: Slip next st to cable needle and place at front of work, p1, then k1 tbl from cable needle.
1/1 RPT: Slip next st to cable needle and place at back of work, k1 tbl, then p1 from cable needle.

See full list of abbreviations on page 66.

PATTERN NOTES
Sock One and Sock Two each use a different set of charts, as the cables are mirrored.

SOCK ONE

CUFF

Cast on 66 (74, 82) sts. Distribute sts over your needles as desired and join to work in the round, being careful not to twist. Place marker for start of round.

Round 1: Reading from right to left, work from row 1 of chart A, repeating marked section 7 (9, 11) times in total.

Last round sets rib pattern. Work this round 15 more times.

LEG

Round 1: Reading from right to left, work from row 2 of chart A, repeating marked section 7 (9, 11) times in total.
Last round sets chart A pattern.
Continue to work from chart A as set, until row 12 is complete. Then work all 12 rows 4 more times.

HEEL SET-UP

Partial round (omit for Sock Two): *P3, k1 tbl, repeat from * 3 (4, 5) more times.

HEEL FLAP

Turn work so WS is facing. Heel flap will be worked back and forth on the next 33 (37, 41) sts, beginning with a WS row. Keep remaining 33 (37, 41) sts on needles for instep.
Row 1 (WS): Sl1 wyif, [k3, p1 tbl] 3 (4, 5) times, k2, [k1, p2] 6 times.
Row 2 (RS): Sl1 wyib, k1, [p1, k2] 5 times, [p3, k1tbl] 3 (4, 5) times, p3, k1.

Repeat these 2 rows 14 more times then work row 1 once more.

TURN HEEL

Row 1 (RS): Sl1 wyib, k17 (19, 21), ssk, k1, turn, leaving remaining 12 (14, 16) sts unworked.
Row 2: Sl1 wyif, p4, p2tog, p1, turn, leaving remaining 12 (14, 16) sts unworked.
Row 3: Sl1 wyib, k to 1 st before gap, ssk, k1, turn.
Row 4: Sl1 wyif, p to 1 st before gap, p2tog, p1, turn.
Repeat last 2 rows 5 (6, 7) more times. All heel sts have been worked. 19 (21, 23) heel sts remain.

GUSSET

Set-up Round: Sl1, k18 (20, 22), pick up and knit 16 sts along edge of heel flap (1 stitch in each slipped stitch along the edge of the flap), work 33 (37, 41) sts across instep in pattern from row 1 of chart B, repeating marked section 3 (4, 5) times in total, pick up and knit 16 sts along edge of heel flap, k35 (37, 39). Place marker for new start of round (at start of instep stitches). 84 (90, 96) sts.

Round 1: Work from row 2 of chart B, repeating marked section 3 (4, 5) times in total across instep stitches, ssk, k to 2 sts before end of round, k2tog. 82 (88, 94) sts.
Round 2: Work from row 3 of chart B, repeating marked section 3 (4, 5) times in total across instep stitches, k to end of round.
Last 2 rounds set chart B pattern on instep, and gusset decreases. Repeat these 2

Charts

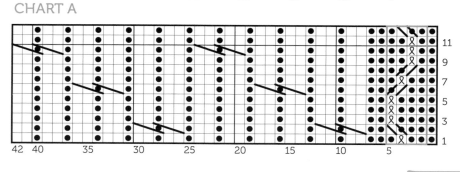

SOCK TWO

CHART D

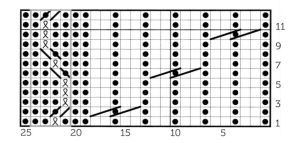

CHART C

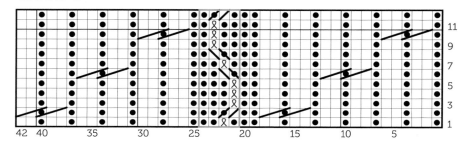

SOCK ONE

CHART B

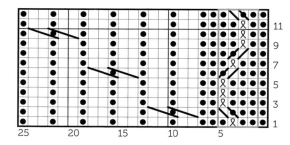

CHART A

KEY

☐	Knit
●	Purl
⚇	K1 tbl
⟋	2/1/2 RPC
⟋	2/1/2 LPC
⟍	1/1 LPT
⟋	1/1 RPT
☐	Pattern repeat

rounds 8 (7, 6) more times, working next row of chart each time. 66 (74, 82) sts.

You should now have 33 (37, 41) sts each on instep and sole.

FOOT
Work as set (chart B on instep sts and st st on sole) without further shaping until sock measures 5cm [2in] less than the desired foot length.

TOE
Round 1: Knit.
Round 2: K1, ssk, k27 (31, 35), k2tog, k1, pm, k1, ssk, k27 (31, 35), k2tog, k1. 62 (70, 78) sts.
Round 3: Knit.
Round 4: *K1, ssk, k to 3 sts before marker, k2tog, k1, slm; repeat from * once more. 58 (66, 74) sts.
Repeat last 2 rounds 10 (11, 13) more times. 18 (22, 22) sts.
Cut yarn, leaving a 30cm [12in] tail. Graft sts together using Kitchener stitch. Weave in ends.

SOCK TWO

CUFF AND LEG
Work as Sock One, using chart C instead of chart A.

HEEL SET-UP
Skip straight to Heel Flap.

HEEL FLAP
Turn work so WS is facing. Heel flap will be worked back and forth on the next 33 (37, 41) sts, beginning with a WS row.
Keep remaining 33 (37, 41) sts on needles for instep.
Row 1 (WS): Sl1 wyif, p1, [k1, p2] 5 times, k3, [p1 tbl, k3] 3 (4, 5) times, p1.
Row 2 (RS): Sl1 wyib, [p3, k1 tbl] 3 (4, 5) times, p3, [k2, p1] 5 times, k2.
Complete Heel flap as for Sock One.

HEEL, FOOT AND TOE
Work as for Sock One to end, using chart D instead of chart B on the instep sts.

elicate, tiny flowers inspired these pretty socks. The lace pattern swirls around leg and foot like a tree full of blossom.

Pennycress

Pennycress

YARN
Madelinetosh Tosh Sock (100% superwash merino;
361m per 100g skein)
Ivy, 1 x 100g skein

NEEDLES
2mm [UK 14/US 0] 80cm [30in] circular needles or
DPNs (or size needed to get gauge)
Tapestry needle
Stitch markers

TENSION
36 sts and 50 rows = 10cm [4in] over st st
33.5 sts and 55 rows = 10cm [4in] over unstretched
lace pattern

SIZES
Small (Medium, Large)
To fit foot circumference:
20 (23, 25.5) cm [8 (9, 10) in]
Actual foot circumference of sock, unstretched:
15.5 (18, 20) cm [6 (7, 8) in]

ABBREVIATIONS
See full list of abbreviations on page 66.

PATTERN NOTES
There are different charts for Sock One and Sock
Two, as the lace pattern is mirrored.
Written instructions for the charts are given on the
following page.

SOCK ONE

CUFF

Cast on 56 (64, 72) sts. Distribute sts over your needles as desired and join to work in the round, being careful not to twist. Place marker for start of round.

Round 1: *K2, p2; repeat from * to end.
Last round sets rib pattern. Work this round 19 more times.

LEG

Round 1: Reading from right to left, work from chart A, repeating 8-stitch motif 7 (8, 9) times in total.
Last round sets chart A pattern. Continue to work in pattern as set until the main chart has been completed 8 times, then work rounds 1-4 once more. A total of 68 rounds have been worked in lace pattern.

HEEL SET-UP

Small and Large sizes only
Chart round 5: Knit to last st. Leave remaining stitch unworked.

Medium size only
Chart round 5: Knit to end of round.
Next round: K1. Leave remaining sts unworked.

All sizes
Continue to Heel Flap.

HEEL FLAP

Turn work so WS is facing. Heel flap will be worked back and forth on the next 29 (33, 37) sts, beginning with a WS row. Keep remaining 27 (31, 35) sts on needles for instep.

Row 1 (WS): Sl1 wyif, p28 (32, 36).
Row 2 (RS): *Sl1 wyib, k1; repeat from * until 1 st remains, k1.
Repeat last 2 rows 14 more times then work row 1 once more.

TURN HEEL

Row 1 (RS): Sl1 wyib, k15 (17, 19), ssk, k1, turn, leaving remaining 10 (12, 14) sts unworked.

Row 2: Sl1 wyif, p4, p2tog, p1, turn, leaving remaining 10 (12, 14) sts unworked.
Row 3: Sl1 wyib, k to 1 st before gap, ssk, k1, turn.
Row 4: Sl1 wyif, p to 1 st before gap, p2tog, p1, turn.
Repeat last 2 rows 4 (5, 6) more times. All heel sts have been worked. 17 (19, 21) heel sts remain.

GUSSET

Set-up Round: Sl1, k16 (18, 20), pick up and knit 16 sts along edge of heel flap (1 stitch in each slipped stitch along the edge of the flap), work across instep sts as foll: reading from right to left, work from row 1 of chart B (C, B), repeating marked section 3 (3, 4) times in total, pick up and knit 16 sts along edge of heel flap, k33 (35, 37).
Place marker for new start of round (at start of instep stitches). 76 (82, 88) sts.
Round 1: Work from row 2 of chart B (C, B), repeating marked section 3 (3, 4) times in total, ssk, k to 2 sts before end of round, k2tog. 74 (80, 86) sts.
Round 2: Work from row 3 of chart B (C, B), repeating marked section 3 (3, 4) times in total, k to end of round.

Last 2 rounds set chart B (C, B) pattern on instep and gusset decreases. Repeat these 2 rounds 10 (9, 8) more times, working next chart row each time. 54 (62, 70) sts.

You should now have 27 (31, 35) sts each on instep and sole.

FOOT

Work as set (chart B (C, B) on instep and st st on sole) without further shaping until sock measures 5cm [2in] less than the desired foot length.

TOE

Round 1: Knit.
Round 2: K1, ssk, k21 (25, 29), k2tog, k1, pm, k1, ssk, k21 (25, 29), k2tog, k1. 50 (58, 66) sts.
Round 3: Knit.
Round 4: *K1, ssk, k to 3 sts before marker, k2tog, k1, slm; repeat from * once more. 46 (54, 62) sts.
Repeat last 2 rounds 7 (8, 10) more times. 18 (22, 22) sts.
Cut yarn, leaving a 30cm [12in] tail. Graft sts together using Kitchener stitch. Weave in ends.

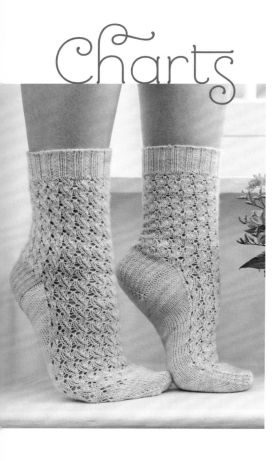

Charts

SOCK TWO

CHART F: SOCK TWO INSTEP
MEDIUM

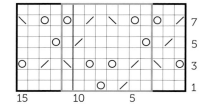

CHART E: SOCK TWO INSTEP
SMALL & LARGE

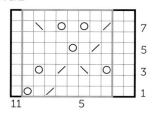

CHART D:
SOCK TWO MAIN

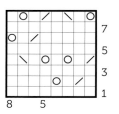

SOCK ONE

CHART C: SOCK ONE INSTEP
MEDIUM

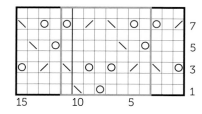

KEY

☐	Knit
◻╲	SSK
◻╱	K2tog
⊙	Yarnover
☐	Pattern repeat

CHART B: SOCK ONE INSTEP
SMALL & LARGE

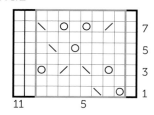

CHART A:
SOCK ONE MAIN

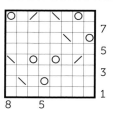

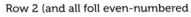

SOCK TWO

CUFF

Cast on 56 (64, 72) sts. Distribute sts over your needles as desired and join to work in the round, being careful not to twist. Place marker for start of round.

Round 1: * P2, k2; repeat from * to end. Last round sets rib pattern. Work this round 19 more times.

LEG

Work as for Sock One, using chart D instead of chart A.

HEEL SET-UP

Small and Large sizes only
Chart round 5: Knit to last 2 sts. Leave remaining 2 sts unworked.

Medium size only
Chart round 5: Knit to end of round.

All sizes
Continue to Heel Flap.

HEEL FLAP AND HEEL TURN

Work as for Sock One.

GUSSET

Set-up Round: Sl1, k16 (18, 20), pick up and knit 16 sts along edge of heel flap (1 stitch in each slipped stitch along the edge of the flap), work across instep sts as foll: reading from right to left, work from row 1 of chart E (F, E), repeating marked section 3 (3, 4) times in total, pick up and knit 16 sts along edge of heel flap, k33 (35, 37).

Place marker for new start of round (at start of instep stitches). 76 (82, 88) sts.

Complete gusset as set, working from charts E (F, E) instead of charts B (C, B).

FOOT

Work as Sock One, using charts E (F, E) instead of charts B (C, B).

TOE

Work as Sock One.

WRITTEN CHART INSTRUCTIONS

CHART A: SOCK ONE MAIN

Row 1 (and all foll odd-numbered rows): K8.
Row 2: K4, yo, k1, ssk, k1.
Row 4: K1, k2tog, k1, yo, k1, yo, k1, ssk.
Row 6: Yo, k1, ssk, k5.
Row 8: K1, yo, k1, ssk, k1, k2tog, k1, yo.

CHART B: SOCK ONE INSTEP
SMALL AND LARGE
Row 1: K1, *yo, k1, ssk, k5; repeat from * 2 (-, 3) more times, k2.
Row 2 (and all foll even-numbered rows): K27 (-, 35).
Row 3: K1, *k1, yo, k1, ssk, k1, k2tog, k1, yo; repeat from * 2 (-, 3) more times, k2.
Row 5: K1, *k4, yo, k1, ssk, k1; repeat from * 2 (-, 3) more times, k2.
Row 7: K1, *k1, k2tog, k1, yo, k1, yo, k1, ssk; repeat from * 2 (-, 3) more times, k2.
Row 8: As row 2.

CHART C: SOCK ONE INSTEP
MEDIUM
Row 1: K3, *k4, yo, k1, ssk, k1; repeat from * 2 more times, k4.
Row 2 (and all foll even-numbered rows): K31.
Row 3: Yo, k1, ssk, *k1, k2tog, k1, yo, k1, yo, k1, ssk; repeat from * 2 more times, k1, k2tog, k1, yo.
Row 5: K3, *yo, k1, ssk, k5; repeat from * 2 more times, yo, k1, ssk, k1.
Row 7: K2tog, k1, yo, *k1, yo, k1, ssk, k1, k2tog, k1, yo; repeat from * 2 more times, k1, yo, k1, ssk.
Row 8: As row 2.

CHART D: SOCK TWO MAIN

Row 1 (and all foll odd-numbered rows): K8.
Row 2: K1, k2tog, k1, yo, k4.
Row 4: K2tog, k1, yo, k1, yo, k1, ssk, k1.
Row 6: K5, k2tog, k1, yo.
Row 8: Yo, k1, ssk, k1, k2tog, k1, yo, k1.

CHART E: SOCK TWO INSTEP
SMALL AND LARGE
Row 1: K2, *k5, ssk, k1, yo; repeat from * 2 (-, 3) more times, k1.

Row 2 (and all foll even-numbered rows): K27 (-, 35).
Row 3: K2, *yo, k1, ssk, k1, k2tog, k1, yo, k1; repeat from * 2 (-, 3) more times, k1.
Row 5: K2, *k1, k2tog, k1, yo, k4; repeat from * 2 (-, 3) more times, k1.
Row 7: K2, *k2tog, k1, yo, k1, yo, k1, ssk, k1; repeat from * 2 (-, 3) more times, k1.
Row 8: As row 2.

CHART F: SOCK TWO INSTEP
MEDIUM
Row 1: K3, *k2, k2tog, k1, yo, k3; repeat from * 2 more times, k4.
Row 2 (and all foll even-numbered rows): K31.
Row 3: Yo, k1, ssk, *k1, k2tog, k1, yo, k1, yo, k1, ssk; repeat from * 2 more times, k1, k2tog, k1, yo.
Row 5: K1, k2tog, k1, *yo, k5, k2tog, k1; repeat from * 2 more times, yo, k3.
Row 7: K2tog, k1, yo, *k1, yo, k1, ssk, k1, k2tog, k1, yo; repeat from * 2 more times, k1, yo, k1, ssk.
Row 8: As row 2.

Sailor stripes decorate cuff and toe, while a cable and texture pattern undulates across these nautical socks.

Saltburn

Saltburn

YARN
The Knitting Goddess Merino and Nylon Sock (75% merino, 25% nylon; 212m per 50g skein)
Colour 1: Semi-solid Slate, 2 x 50g skeins
Colour 2: Semi-solid Silver, 1 x 50g skein

NEEDLES
2.25mm [UK 13/US 1] 80cm [30in] circular needles or DPNs (or size needed to get gauge)
Cable needle
Tapestry needle
Stitch markers

TENSION
36 sts and 50 rows = 10cm [4in] over st st
39 sts and 52 rows = 10cm [4in] over unstretched cable patterns

SIZES
Small (Medium, Large)
To fit foot circumference:
20 (23, 25.5) cm [8 (9, 10) in]
Actual foot circumference of sock, unstretched:
16.5 (19, 21.5) cm [6.5 (7.5, 8.5) in]

ABBREVIATION
2/1 RPC: Slip next st to cable needle and place at back of work, k2, then p1 from cable needle
2/1 LPC: Slip next 2 sts to cable needle and place at front of work, p1, then k2 from cable needle
2/2 RC: Slip next 2 sts to cable needle and place at back of work, k2, then k2 from cable needle
2/2 LC: Slip next 2 sts to cable needle and place at front of work, k2, then k2 from cable needle

See full list of abbreviations on page 66.

PATTERN NOTES
There are different charts for Sock One and Sock Two, as the patterns are mirrored.
Written instructions for the charts are given on the following page.

SOCK ONE

CUFF

With colour 2, cast on 63 (72, 81) sts. Distribute sts over your needles as desired and join to work in the round, being careful not to twist. Place marker for start of round.

Rounds 1 and 2: Using colour 2, *k1 tbl, p1, k2, p2, k2, p1; repeat from * to end.
Round 3: Using colour 1, work as round 1.
Round 4: Using colour 2, work as round 1.
Last 4 rounds set striped rib pattern. Repeat these 4 rounds 3 more times, then work rounds 1 and 2 once more.

Round 19: Using colour 1 and reading from right to left, work from row 1 of chart A, repeating the 9-stitch motif 7 (8, 9) times in total.

LEG

Round 1: Using colour 1 and reading from right to left, work from row 1 of chart B, repeating the 9-stitch motif 7 (8, 9) times in total.
Last round sets main pattern, which is worked in colour 1 throughout. Continue to work as set until chart B has been completed 5 times, then work rounds 1 to 6 once more. A total of 56 rounds in chart B pattern have been worked.

HEEL SET-UP
Small and Large sizes only
Chart round 7: Work round 7 of chart B to last 2 sts. Leave remaining 2 stitches unworked.

Medium size only
Chart round 7: Work round 7 of chart B.
Next round: K1. Leave remaining sts unworked.

All sizes
Continue to Heel Flap.

HEEL FLAP

Turn work so WS is facing. Heel flap will be worked back and forth on the next 31 (37, 40) sts, beginning with a WS row. Keep remaining 32 (35, 41) sts on needles for instep.

Row 1 (WS): Sl1 wyif, p30 (36, 39).
Row 2 (RS): *Sl1 wyib, k1; repeat from * until 1 st remains, k1.
Repeat last 2 rows 14 more times then work row 1 once more.

TURN HEEL

Row 1 (RS): Sl1 wyib, k17 (19, 22), ssk, k1, turn, leaving remaining 10 (14, 14) sts unworked.
Row 2: Sl1 wyif, p6 (4, 7), p2tog, p1, turn, leaving remaining 10 (14, 14) sts unworked.
Row 3: Sl1 wyib, k to 1 st before gap, ssk, k1, turn.
Row 4: Sl1 wyif, p to 1 st before gap, p2tog, p1, turn.
Repeat last 2 rows 4 (6, 6) more times.

All heel sts have been worked. 19 (21, 24) heel sts remain.

GUSSET

Set-up Round: Sl1, k18 (20, 23), pick up and knit 16 sts along edge of heel flap (1 stitch in each slipped stitch along the edge of the flap), work across instep sts as foll: reading from right to left, work from row 1 of chart C (D, C), repeating marked section 3 (3, 4) times in total, pick up and knit 16 sts along edge of heel flap, k35 (37, 40). Place marker for new start of round (at start of instep stitches). 83 (88, 97) sts.

Round 1: Reading from right to left, work from row 2 of chart C (D, C), repeating marked section 3 (3, 4) times in total, ssk, k to 2 sts before end of round, k2tog. 81 (86, 95) sts.
Round 2: Reading from right to left, work from row 3 of chart C (D, C), repeating marked section 3 (3, 4) times in total, k to end of round.

Last 2 rounds set chart C (D, C) pattern on instep and gusset decreases. Repeat these 2 rounds 9 (8, 7) more times, working next row of chart each time. 63 (70, 81) sts.

Small and Large sizes only
Next round: Work in pattern across instep stitches, ssk, k to end. 62 (-, 80) sts.

All sizes
You should now have 32 (35, 41) sts on instep and 30 (35, 39) sts on sole.

FOOT

Work as set (chart C (D, C) pattern on instep and st st on sole) without further shaping until sock measures 5cm [2in] less than the desired foot length.

TOE
Small and Large sizes only
Next round: K1, ssk, k26 (-, 35), k2tog, k1, pm, k to end. 60 (-, 78) sts.

Medium size only
Next round: K35, pm, k to end.

All sizes
Round 1: Using colour 2, knit.
Round 2: Using colour 2, *k1, ssk, k to 3 sts before marker, k2tog, k1, slm; repeat from * once more. 56 (66, 74) sts.
Round 3: Using colour 2, knit.
Round 4: Using colour 1, *k1, ssk, k to 3 sts before marker, k2tog, k1, slm; repeat from * once more. 52 (62, 70) sts.
Repeat last 4 rounds 4 (5, 6) more times. 20 (22, 22) sts.

Cut yarn, leave a 30cm [12in] tail of colour 2. Using colour 2, graft sts together using Kitchener stitch. Weave in ends.

Charts

CHART A: CUFF
SOCKS ONE AND TWO

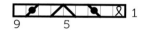

SOCK TWO

CHART G: INSTEP MEDIUM

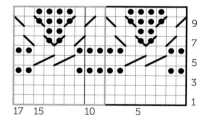

CHART F: INSTEP
SMALL AND LARGE

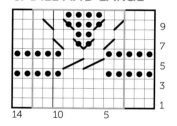

CHART E: MAIN

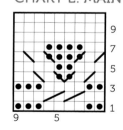

KEY

☐	Knit
●	Purl
⊠	K1 tbl
↗	2/1 RPC
↘	2/1 LPC
⟋	2/2 RC
⟍	2/2 LC
☐	Pattern repeat

SOCK ONE

CHART D: INSTEP MEDIUM

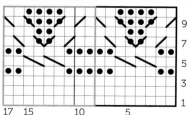

CHART C: INSTEP
SMALL AND LARGE

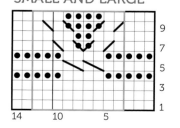

CHART B: MAIN

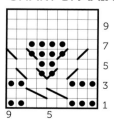

SOCK TWO
CUFF

Work as Sock One.

LEG

Round 1: Using colour 1 and reading from right to left, work from row 1 of chart E, repeating the 9-stitch motif 7 (8, 9) times in total.

Last round sets main pattern, which is worked in colour 1 throughout. Continue to work as set until chart E has been completed 5 times, then work rounds 1 to 6 once more. A total of 56 rounds in chart E pattern have been worked.

HEEL SET-UP

Small and Large sizes only
Chart round 7: Work round 7 of chart E to last 3 sts. Leave remaining 3 stitches unworked.

Medium size only
Chart round 7: Work round 7 of chart E.

All sizes
Continue to Heel Flap.

HEEL FLAP AND HEEL TURN

Work as Sock One.

GUSSET

Set-up Round: Sl1, k18 (20, 23), pick up and knit 16 sts along edge of heel flap (1 stitch in each slipped stitch along the edge of the flap), work across instep sts as foll: reading from right to left, work from row 1 of chart F (G, F), repeating marked section 3 (3, 4) times in total, pick up and knit 16 sts along edge of heel flap, k35 (37, 40). Place marker for new start of round (at start of instep stitches). 83 (88, 97) sts.

Complete gusset as for Sock One, using chart F (G, F) instead of chart C (D, C).

FOOT

Work as Sock One, but using chart F (G, F) instead of chart C (D, C).

TOE

Work as Sock One.

WRITTEN CHART INSTRUCTIONS

CHART A: CUFF
Row 1: K1 tbl, k1, 2/1 LPC, 2/1 RPC, k1.

CHART B: SOCK ONE MAIN
Row 1: P3, k4, p2.
Row 2: K3, 2/2 LC, k2.
Row 3: As row 1.
Row 4: K2, 2/1 RPC, 2/1 LPC, k1.
Row 5: K4, p2, k3.
Row 6: K1, 2/1 RPC, p2, 2/1 LPC.
Row 7: K3, p4, k2.
Rows 8-10: K9.

CHART C: SOCK ONE INSTEP SMALL AND LARGE
Rows 1-3: K32 (-, 41).
Row 4: P3, *p2, k4, p3; repeat from * 2 (-, 3) more times, p2.
Row 5: K3, *k2, 2/2 LC, k3; repeat from * 2 (-, 3) more times, k2.
Row 6: As row 4.
Row 7: K3, *k1, 2/1 RPC, 2/1 LPC, k2; repeat from * 2 (-, 3) more times, k2.
Row 8: K3, *k3, p2, k4; repeat from * 2 (-, 3) more times, k2.
Row 9: K3, *2/1 RPC, p2, 2/1 LPC, k1; repeat from * 2 (-, 3) more times, k2.
Row 10: K3, *k2, p4, k3; repeat from * 2 (-, 3) more times, k2.

CHART D: SOCK ONE INSTEP MEDIUM
Rows 1-3: K35.
Row 4: P2, k4, p2, *p3, k4, p2; repeat from * 2 more times.
Row 5: K2, 2/2 LC, k2, *k3, 2/2 LC, k2; repeat from * 2 more times.
Row 6: As row 4.
Row 7: K1, 2/1 RPC, 2/1 LPC, k1, *k2, 2/1 RPC, 2/1 LPC, k1; repeat from * 2 more times.
Row 8: K3, p2, k3, *k4, p2, k3; repeat from * 2 more times.
Row 9: 2/1 RPC, p2, 2/1 LPC, *k1, 2/1 RPC, p2, 2/1 LPC; repeat from * 2 more times.
Row 10: K2, p4, k2, *k3, p4, k2; repeat from * 2 more times.

CHART E: SOCK TWO MAIN
Row 1: P2, k4, p3.
Row 2: K2, 2/2 LC, k3.
Row 3: As row 1.
Row 4: K1, 2/1 RPC, 2/1 LPC, k2.
Row 5: K3, p2, k4.
Row 6: 2/1 RPC, p2, 2/1 LPC, k1.
Row 7: K2, p4, k3.
Rows 8-10: K9.

CHART F: SOCK TWO INSTEP SMALL AND LARGE
Rows 1-3: K32 (-, 41).
Row 4: P3, *p2, k4, p3; repeat from * 2 (-, 3) more times, p2.
Row 5: K3, *k2, 2/2 RC, k3; repeat from * 2 (-, 3) more times, k2.
Row 6: As row 4.
Row 7: K3, *k1, 2/1 RPC, 2/1 LPC, k2; repeat from * 2 (-, 3) more times, k2.
Row 8: K3, *k3, p2, k4; repeat from * 2 (-, 3) more times, k2.
Row 9: K3, *2/1 RPC, p2, 2/1 LPC, k1; repeat from * 2 (-, 3) more times, k2.
Row 10: K3, *k2, p4, k3; repeat from * 2 (-, 3) more times, k2.

CHART G: SOCK TWO INSTEP MEDIUM
Rows 1-3: K35.
Row 4: P2, k4, p2, *p3, k4, p2; repeat from * 2 more times.
Row 5: K2, 2/2 RC, k2, *k3, 2/2 RC, k2; repeat from * 2 more times.
Row 6: As row 4.
Row 7: K1, 2/1 RPC, 2/1 LPC, k1, *k2, 2/1 RPC, 2/1 LPC, k1; repeat from * 2 more times.
Row 8: K3, p2, k3, *k4, p2, k3; repeat from * 2 more times.
Row 9: 2/1 RPC, p2, 2/1 LPC, *k1, 2/1 RPC, p2, 2/1 LPC; repeat from * 2 more times.
Row 10: K2, p4, k2, *k3, p4, k2; repeat from * 2 more times.

Calamint

A cascade of lace petals and twisted stitches tumble down these socks towards the toe.

Calamint

YARN
Socktopus Sokkusu O (100% superwash merino;
396m per 120g skein)
Summer Crush, 1 x 120g skein

NEEDLES
2.25mm [UK 13/US 1] 80cm [30in] circular needles
or DPNs (or size needed to get gauge)
Tapestry needle
Stitch markers

TENSION
36 sts and 50 rows = 10cm [4in] over st st
36 sts and 50 rows = 10cm [4in] over unstretched
lace pattern and twisted rib

SIZES
Small (Medium, Large)
To fit foot circumference:
20 (23, 25.5) cm [8 (9, 10) in]
Actual foot circumference of sock, unstretched:
15.5 (18, 20) cm [6 (7, 8) in]

ABBREVIATIONS
See full list of abbreviations on page 66.

PATTERN NOTES
Sock One and Sock Two are worked alike.
Written instructions for charts are given on the
following page.

BOTH SOCKS

CUFF

Cast on 56 (64, 72) sts. Distribute sts over your needles as desired and join to work in the round, being careful not to twist. Place marker for start of round.

Round 1: *P1, k4, [p1, k1 tbl] 2 (3, 4) times, p1, k4; repeat from * to end.
Last round sets rib pattern. Work this round 2 more times.

LEG

Round 1: Reading from right to left, *work from row 1 of chart A, repeating marked section 1 (2, 3) times in total; repeat from * to end.
Last round sets chart A pattern. Continue to work from chart A until row 6 is complete, then work rows 1-6 a further 5 times, followed by rows 1-4 once more. A total of 40 rounds have been worked in chart A pattern.

Round 41: Reading from right to left, *work from row 1 of chart B, repeating marked section 1 (2, 3) times in total; repeat from * to end.
Last round sets chart B pattern. Continue to work from chart B until row 6 is complete, then work rows 1-6 a further 5 times. A total of 36 rounds have been worked in chart B pattern.

HEEL FLAP

Turn work so WS is facing. Heel flap will be worked back and forth on the next 27 (31, 35) sts, beginning with a WS row.
Keep remaining 29 (33, 37) sts on needles for instep.
Row 1 (WS): Sl1 wyif, p3, [k1, p1 tbl] 2 (3, 4) times, [k1, p4] twice, [k1, p1 tbl] 2 (3, 4) times, k1, p4.
Row 2 (RS): Sl1 wyib, k3, [p1, k1 tbl] 2 (3, 4) times, [p1, k4] twice, [p1, k1 tbl] 2 (3, 4) times, p1, k4.
Repeat last 2 rows 14 more times then work row 1 once more.

TURN HEEL

Row 1 (RS): Sl1 wyib, k15 (17, 19), ssk, k1, turn, leaving remaining 8 (10, 12) sts unworked.
Row 2: Sl1 wyif, p6, p2tog, p1, turn, leaving remaining 8 (10, 12) sts unworked.
Row 3: Sl1 wyib, k to 1 st before gap, ssk, k1, turn.

Row 4: Sl1 wyif, p to 1 st before gap, p2tog, p1, turn.
Repeat last 2 rows 3 (4, 5) more times. All heel sts have been worked. 17 (19, 21) heel sts remain.

GUSSET

Set-up Round: Sl1, k16 (18, 20), pick up and knit 16 sts along edge of heel flap (1 stitch in each slipped stitch along the edge of the flap), work across instep sts as foll: reading from right to left, work from row 1 of chart C, repeating the marked sections 1 (2, 3) times in total, on each side of the centre motif, pick up and knit 16 sts along edge of heel flap, k33 (35, 37).

Place marker for new start of round (at start of instep stitches). 78 (84, 90) sts.

Round 1: Reading from right to left, work from row 2 of chart C, repeating the marked sections 1 (2, 3) times in total, on each side of the centre motif, ssk, k to 2 sts before end of round, k2tog. 76 (82, 88) sts.
Round 2: Reading from right to left, work from row 3 of chart C, repeating the marked sections 1 (2, 3) times in total,

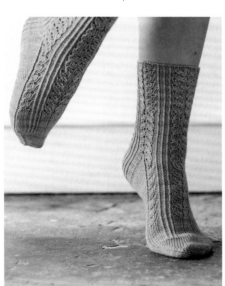

Charts

CHART C: INSTEP

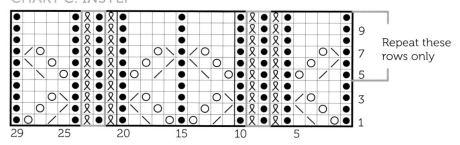

Repeat these rows only

KEY

☐	Knit
●	Purl
℞	K1 tbl
＼	SSK
／	K2tog
○	Yarnover
☐	Pattern repeat

CHART B

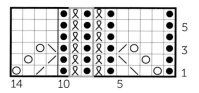

CHART A

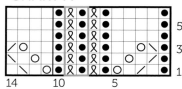

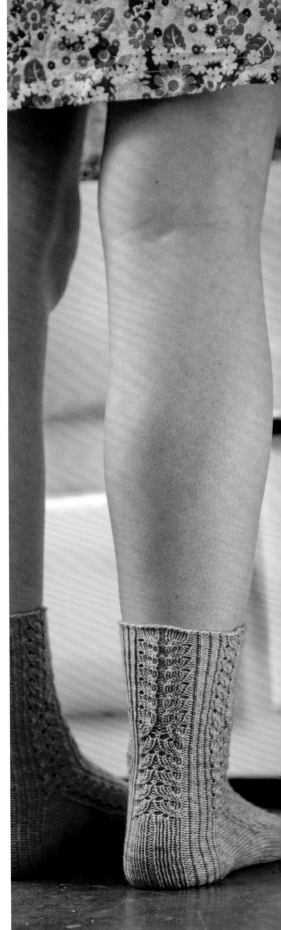

on each side of the centre motif, k to end of round.

Last 2 rounds set chart C pattern on instep and gusset decreases. Repeat these 2 rounds 10 (9, 8) more times, working next row of chart until chart row 10 is complete, then repeating rows 5-10 only. 56 (64, 72) sts.

You should now have 29 (33, 37) sts on instep and 27 (31, 35) sts on sole.

FOOT

Work as set (chart C on instep and st st on sole) until rows 5-10 of chart C have been repeated 7 times in total, then repeat row 10 only, until sock measures 5cm [2in] less than the desired foot length.

TOE

Round 1: K1, ssk, k23 (27, 31), k2tog, k1, pm, k to end. 54 (62, 70) sts.
Round 2: Knit.
Round 3: *K1, ssk, k to 3 sts before marker, k2tog, k1, slm; repeat from * once more. 50 (58, 66) sts.
Repeat last 2 rounds 8 (9, 11) more times. 18 (22, 22) sts.
Cut yarn, leaving a 30cm [12in] tail. Graft sts together using Kitchener stitch. Weave in ends.

WRITTEN CHART INSTRUCTIONS

CHART A

Row 1: P1, k1, k2tog, k1, yo, p1, k1 tbl, *p1, k1 tbl; repeat from * 0 (1, 2) more times, p1, yo, k1, ssk, k1.
Row 2: P1, k2tog, k1, yo, k1, p1, k1 tbl, *p1, k1 tbl; repeat from * 0 (1, 2) more times, p1, k1, yo, k1, ssk.
Row 3: P1, ssk, yo, k2, p1, k1 tbl, *p1, k1 tbl; repeat from * 0 (1, 2) more times, p1, k2, yo, k2tog.
Rows 4-6: P1, k4, p1, k1 tbl, *p1, k1 tbl; repeat from * 0 (1, 2) more times, p1, k4.

CHART B

Row 1: P1, yo, k1, ssk, k1, p1, k1 tbl, *p1, k1 tbl; repeat from * 0 (1, 2) more times, p1, k1, k2tog, k1, yo.

Row 2: P1, k1, yo, k1, ssk, p1, k1 tbl, *p1, k1 tbl; repeat from * 0 (1, 2) more times, p1, k2tog, k1, yo, k1.
Row 3: P1, k2, yo, k2tog, p1, k1 tbl, *p1, k1 tbl; repeat from * 0 (1, 2) more times, p1, ssk, yo, k2.
Rows 4-6: P1, k4, p1, k1 tbl, *p1, k1 tbl; repeat from * 0 (1, 2) more times, p1, k4.

CHART C: INSTEP

Row 1: P1, yo, k1, ssk, k1, p1, k1 tbl, *p1, k1 tbl; repeat from * 0 (1, 2) more times, p1, k1, k2tog, k1, yo, p1, yo, k1, ssk, k1, p1, k1 tbl, *p1, k1 tbl; repeat from * 0 (1, 2) more times, p1, k1, k2tog, k1, yo, p1.
Row 2: P1, k1, yo, k1, ssk, p1, k1 tbl, *p1, k1 tbl; repeat from * 0 (1, 2) more times, p1, k2tog, k1, yo, k1, p1, k1, yo, k1, ssk, p1, k1 tbl, *p1, k1 tbl; repeat from * 0 (1, 2) more times, p1, k2tog, k1, yo, k1, p1.
Row 3: P1, k2, yo, k2tog, p1, k1 tbl, *p1, k1 tbl; repeat from * 0 (1, 2) more times, p1, ssk, yo, k2, p1, k2, yo, k2tog, p1, k1 tbl, *p1, k1 tbl; repeat from * 0 (1, 2) more times, p1, ssk, yo, k2, p1.
Row 4: P1, k4, p1, k1 tbl, *p1, k1 tbl; repeat from * 0 (1, 2) more times, p1, k4, p1, k4, p1, k1 tbl, *p1, k1 tbl; repeat from * 0 (1, 2) more times, p1, k4, p1.
Row 5: P1, k1, k2tog, k1, yo, p1, k1 tbl, *p1, k1 tbl; repeat from * 0 (1, 2) more times, p1, yo, k1, ssk, k1, p1, k1, k2tog, k1, yo, p1, k1 tbl, *p1, k1 tbl; repeat from * 0 (1, 2) more times, p1, yo, k1, ssk, k1, p1.
Row 6: P1, k2tog, k1, yo, k1, p1, k1 tbl, *p1, k1 tbl; repeat from * 0 (1, 2) more times, p1, k1, yo, k1, ssk, p1, k2tog, k1, yo, k1, p1, k1 tbl, *p1, k1 tbl; repeat from * 0 (1, 2) more times, p1, k1, yo, k1, ssk, p1.
Row 7: P1, ssk, yo, k2, p1, k1 tbl, *p1, k1 tbl; repeat from * 0 (1, 2) more times, p1, k2, yo, k2tog, p1, ssk, yo, k2, p1, k1 tbl, *p1, k1 tbl; repeat from * 0 (1, 2) more times, p1, k2, yo, k2tog, p1.
Rows 8-10: P1, k4, p1, k1 tbl, *p1, k1 tbl; repeat from * 0 (1, 2) more times, p1, k4, p1, k4, p1, k1 tbl, *p1, k1 tbl; repeat from * 0 (1, 2) more times, p1, k4, p1.
Now repeat rows 5-10 only.

Inspired by traditional fisher-men's jumpers, these socks have columns of cables and a clever afterthought heel.

Paignton

Paignton

YARN
Blue Moon Fiber Arts Socks That Rock Lightweight
(100% superwash merino; 370m per 155g skein)
Nyame, 1 (2, 2) x 155g skeins

NEEDLES
2.25mm [UK 13/US 1] 80cm [30in] circular needles
or DPNs (or size needed to get gauge)
Cable needle
Tapestry needle
Stitch markers
Small quantity of 4ply waste yarn in a contrasting
colour

TENSION
32 sts and 44 rows = 10cm [4in] over st st
40 sts and 50 rows = 10cm [4in] over unstretched
cable patterns

SIZES
Small (Medium, Large)
To fit foot circumference:
20 (23, 25.5) cm [8 (9, 10) in]
Actual foot circumference of sock, unstretched:
19 (21, 23) cm [7.5 (8.25, 9) in]

ABBREVIATIONS
2/2 RC: Slip next 2 sts to cable needle and place at
back of work, k2, then k2 from cable needle
2/2 LC: Slip next 2 sts to cable needle and place at
front of work, k2, then k2 from cable needle
2/2 RPC: Slip next 2 sts to cable needle and place at
back of work, k2, then p2 from cable needle
2/2 LPC: Slip next sts to cable needle and place at
front of work, p2, then k2 from cable needle

See full list of abbreviations on page 66.

PATTERN NOTES
Both socks are worked alike, using an afterthought
heel. Instructions on how to work the afterthought
heel are given in the "How to..." section on page 67.

BOTH SOCKS

CUFF

Cast on 72 (80, 88) sts. Distribute sts over your needles as desired and join to work in the round, being careful not to twist. Place marker for start of round.

Round 1: *Reading from right to left *across all charts*, work from row 1 of chart A over 6 sts, p2 (3, 3), k2 (2, 4), p2 (3, 3), work from row 1 of chart B over 12 sts, p2 (3, 3), k2 (2, 4), p2 (3, 3), work from row 1 of chart C over 6 sts; repeat from * once more.
Last round sets rib pattern. Work this round 15 more times.

LEG

Next round: *Reading from right to left *across all charts*, work from row 2 of chart A over 6 sts, p2 (3, 3), k2 (2, 4), p2 (3, 3), work from row 2 of chart B over 12 sts, p2 (3, 3), k2 (2, 4), p2 (3, 3), work from row 2 of chart C over 6 sts; repeat from * once more.
Last round sets chart patterns and rib. Work as set until chart row 10 is complete. Then work chart rows 1-10 three more times.

Next round: Reading from right to left *across all charts*, work from row 1 of chart A over 6 sts, p2 (3, 3), k2 (2, 4), p2 (3, 3), work from row 1 of chart B over 12 sts, p2 (3, 3), k2 (2, 4), p2 (3, 3), work from row 1 of chart C over 6 sts, work from row 1 of chart D (E, F) over remaining 36 (40, 44) sts of the round.
Last round sets new chart patterns and rib. Work as set until chart D (E, F) row 20 (22, 24) is complete.

HEEL SET-UP

Next round: Reading from right to left *across all charts*, work from row 1 (3, 5) of chart A over 6 sts, p2 (3, 3), k2 (2, 4), p2 (3, 3), work from row 1 (3, 5) of chart B over 12 sts, p2 (3, 3), k2 (2, 4), p2 (3, 3), work from row 1 (3, 5) of chart C over 6 sts, use a piece of waste yarn to knit 36 (40, 44) sts to end of round.
Slip these 36 (40, 44) sts back on to left needle and then knit them again with the working yarn.

You will now have 36 (40, 44) sts of waste yarn in your fabric. After completion of the toe, you will return to these sts, unpick the waste yarn and work an 'afterthought' heel. (For a step-by-step photo tutorial for this technique, please see page 67.)

FOOT

Next round: Reading from right to left *across all charts*, work from row 2 (4, 6) of chart A over 6 sts, p2 (3, 3), k2 (2, 4), p2 (3, 3), work from row 2 (4, 6) of chart B over 12 sts, p2 (3, 3), k2 (2, 4), p2 (3, 3), work from row 2 (4, 6) of chart C over 6 sts, knit to end.
Last round sets chart patterns and rib on instep sts, and st st on sole sts. Continue to work as set until charts A, B & C have been completed 9 times in total (for foot lengths of less than 23cm [9in], work 8 repeats in total).

Next round: Work from row 1 of chart D (E, F) over 36 (40, 44) sts, knit to end.

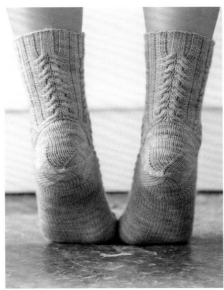

CHART F: LARGE

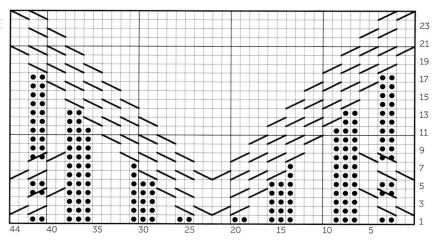

CHART E: MEDIUM

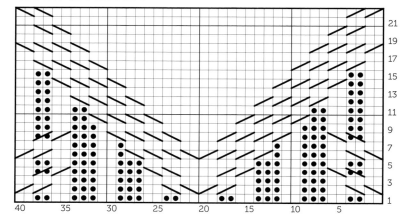

CHART D: SMALL

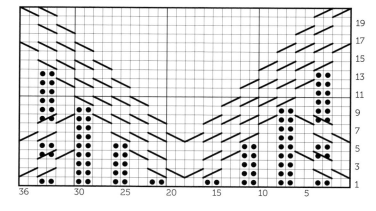

KEY:

☐ Knit

● Purl

2/2 RC

2/2 LC

2/2 RPC

2/2 LPC

Charts

CHART C

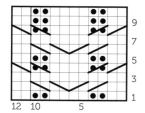

CHART B

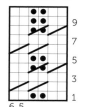

CHART A

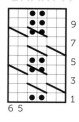

Last round sets chart D (E, F) pattern on instep sts and st st on sole sts. Continue to work as set until chart D (E, F) row 20 (22, 24) is complete.

Now work in st st (knit all sts) until sock measures 11.5cm [4.5in] less than the desired foot length when measured from the row of waste yarn sts.

TOE

Round 1: K1, ssk, k30 (34, 38), k2tog, k1, pm, k1, ssk, k30 (34, 38), k2tog, k1. 68 (76, 84) sts.
Round 2: Knit.
Round 3: *K1, ssk, k to 3 sts before marker, k2tog, k1, slm; repeat from * once more. 64 (72, 80) sts.

Repeat last 2 rounds 10 (12, 14) more times. 24 sts.
Cut yarn, leaving a 30cm [12in] tail. Graft sts together using Kitchener stitch. Weave in ends.

AFTERTHOUGHT HEEL

Pick up the right leg (or side) of the 36 (40, 44) main yarn sts under the row of waste yarn sts. Turn the sock and repeat the process again, picking up 36 (40, 44) sts from the other side of the waste yarn. You should now have 72 (80, 88) stitches on your needles. Carefully remove the waste yarn, ensuring all sts are safely on your needles. Begin to work in the round.

Round 1: K36 (40, 44), pick up and knit 2 stitches in the gap between the sole and instep, k36 (40, 44), pick up 2 stitches in the gap between the sole and instep. 76 (84, 92) sts.

Small size only
Next round: *K17, k2tog; repeat from * to end. 72 sts.

Large size only
Next Round: *K9, k2tog, k10, k2tog; repeat from * to end. 84 sts.

All sizes
Knit 5 (6, 5) rounds. 72 (84, 84) sts.

SHAPE HEEL

Round 1: *K10, k2tog; repeat from * to end. 66 (77, 77) sts.
Round 2: Knit.
Round 3: * K9, k2tog; repeat from * to end. 60 (70, 70) sts.
Round 4: Knit.
Round 5: * K8, k2tog; repeat from * to end. 54 (63, 63) sts.
Round 6: Knit.
Round 7: * K7, k2tog; repeat from * to end. 48 (56, 56) sts.
Round 8: Knit.
Round 9: * K6, k2tog; repeat from * to end. 42 (49, 49) sts.
Round 10: Knit.
Round 11: * K5, k2tog; repeat from * to end. 36 (42, 42) sts.
Round 12: Knit.
Round 13: * K4, k2tog; repeat from * to end. 30 (35, 35) sts.
Round 14: Knit.
Round 15: * K3, k2tog; repeat from * to end. 24 (28, 28) sts.
Round 16: Knit.
Round 17: * K2, k2tog; repeat from * to end. 18 (21, 21) sts.
Round 18: Knit.
Round 19: * K1, k2tog; repeat from * to end. 12 (14, 14) sts.
Round 20: Knit.
Round 21: *K2tog; repeat from * to end. 6 (7, 7) sts.

Break the yarn, leaving a 15cm [6in] tail, thread tail through the remaining stitches and pull tightly to close the heel. Weave in the ends.

Make another sock in the same way.

Willowherb

arn in a wonderful, velvety colour and non-uniform petals combined to inspire this lace and twisted stitch pattern.

Willow Herb

YARN
Fyberspates Vivacious 4ply (100% superwash merino; 365m per 100g skein)
Mixed Magentas (611), 1 x 100g skein

NEEDLES
2.25mm [UK 13/US 1] 80cm [30in] circular needles or DPNs (or size needed to get gauge)
Tapestry needle
Stitch markers

TENSION
36 sts and 50 rows = 10cm [4in] over st st
34.5 sts and 52 rows = 10cm [4in] over unstretched lace and twisted stitch patterns

SIZES
Small (Large)
To fit foot circumference: 20 (25.5) cm [8 (10) in]
Actual foot circumference of sock, unstretched: 18 (21.5) cm [7 (8.5) in]

ABBREVIATIONS
See full list of abbreviations on page 66.

PATTERN NOTES
Written instructions for the charts are given on the following page.

SOCK ONE

CUFF

Cast on 64 (72) sts. Distribute sts over your needles as desired and join to work in the round, being careful not to twist. Place marker for start of round.

Small size only
Round 1: *P1, k1 tbl; repeat from * to end.

Large size only
Round 1: *P2, k1 tbl, [p1, k1 tbl] 3 times; repeat from * to end.

Both sizes
Last round sets rib pattern. Work this round 15 more times.

LEG

Round 1: *P1 (2), reading from right to left, work from row 1 of chart over 7 sts; repeat from * to end.
Round 2: *P1 (2), reading from right to left, work from row 2 of chart over 7 sts; repeat from * to end.
Last 2 rounds set reverse st st and chart patterns. Work as set until chart row 54 is complete, then work chart rows 1-15 once more.

HEEL FLAP

Turn work so WS is facing. Heel flap will be worked back and forth on the next 31 (34) sts, beginning with a WS row. Keep remaining 33 (38) sts on needles for instep.

Small size only
Row 1 (WS): Sl1 wyif, p30.
Row 2 (RS): *Sl1 wyib, k1; repeat from * until 1 st remains, k1.

Large size only
Row 1 (WS): Sl1 wyif, p33.
Row 2 (RS): *[Sl1 wyib, k1] 3 times, sl1 wyib, k2; repeat from * 2 more times, [sl1 wyib, k1] twice, sl1 wyib, k2.

Both sizes
Repeat last 2 rows 14 more times then work row 1 once more.

TURN HEEL

Row 1 (RS): Sl1 wyib, k17 (18), ssk, k1, turn, leaving remaining 10 (12) sts unworked.
Row 2: Sl1 wyif, p6 (5), p2tog, p1, turn, leaving remaining 10 (12) sts unworked.
Row 3: Sl1 wyib, k to 1 st before gap, ssk, k1, turn.
Row 4: Sl1 wyif, p to 1 st before gap, p2tog, p1, turn.
Repeat last 2 rows 4 (5) more times. All heel sts have been worked. 19 (20) heel sts remain.

GUSSET

Set-up Round: Sl1, k18 (19), pick up and knit 16 sts along edge of heel flap (1 stitch in each slipped stitch along the edge of the flap), work across instep sts as foll: *P1 (2), work from chart row 16 over 7 sts; repeat from * 3 more times, p1 (2), pick up and knit 16 sts along edge of heel flap, k35 (36). Place marker for new start of round (at start of instep stitches). 84 (90) sts.

Pattern continues on page 53.

Chart

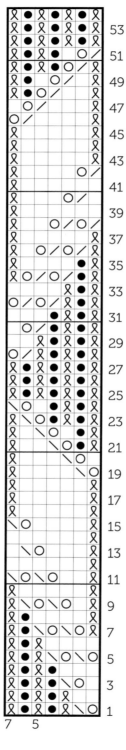

CHART

53
51
49
47
45
43
41
39
37
35
33
31
29
27
25
23
21
19
17
15
13
11
9
7
5
3
1

7   5

KEY

□	Knit
●	Purl
⅄	K1 tbl
╲	SSK
╱	K2tog
O	Yarnover

WRITTEN CHART INSTRUCTIONS

CHART

Row 1: Yo, ssk, [K1 tbl, p1] 2 times, k1 tbl.
Row 2: K2, [k1 tbl, p1] 2 times, k1 tbl.
Row 3: K1, yo, ssk, [p1, k1 tbl] 2 times.
Row 4: K3, [p1, k1 tbl] 2 times.
Row 5: [Yo, ssk] 2 times, k1 tbl, p1, k1 tbl.
Row 6: K4, k1 tbl, p1,k1 tbl.
Row 7: K1 tbl, [yo, ssk] 2 times, p1, k1 tbl.
Row 8: K1 tbl, k4, p1, k1 tbl.
Row 9: K1 tbl, k1, [yo, ssk] 2 times, k1 tbl.
Row 10: K1 tbl, k5, k1 tbl.
Row 11: K1 tbl, k2, [yo ssk] 2 times.
Row 12: K1 tbl, k6.
Row 13: K1 tbl, k3, yo, ssk, k1.
Row 14: As row 12.
Row 15: K1 tbl, k4, yo, ssk.
Rows 16-18: As row 10.
Row 19: Yo, ssk, k4, k1 tbl.
Row 20: K1, yo, ssk, k3, k1 tbl.
Row 21: K1 tbl, p1, yo, skk, k2, k1 tbl.
Row 22: K1 tbl, p1, k1, yo, ssk, k1, k1 tbl.
Row 23: [K1 tbl, p1] 2 times, yo, ssk, k1 tbl.
Row 24: [K1 tbl, p1] 2 times, k1, yo, ssk.
Rows 25-27: [K1 tbl, p1] 3 times, k1 tbl.
Row 28: [K1 tbl, p1] 2 times, k1 tbl, k2tog, yo.
Row 29: [K1 tbl, p1] 2 times, k1 tbl, k2.
Row 30: [K1 tbl, p1] 2 times, k2tog, yo, k1.
Row 31: [K1 tbl, p1] 2 times, k3.
Row 32: K1 tbl, p1, k1 tbl, [k2tog, yo] 2 times.
Row 33: K1 tbl, p1, k1 tbl, k4.
Row 34: K1 tbl, p1, [k2tog yo] 2 times, k1 tbl.
Row 35: K1 tbl, p1, k4, k1 tbl.
Row 36: K1 tbl, [k2tog yo] 2 times, k1, k1 tbl.
Row 37: K1 tbl, k5, k1 tbl.
Row 38: [K2tog, yo] 2 times, k2, k1 tbl.
Row 39: K6, k1 tbl.
Row 40: K1, k2tog, yo, k3, k1 tbl.
Row 41: As row 39.
Row 42: K2tog, yo, k4, k1 tbl.
Rows 43-45: As row 37.
Row 46: K1 tbl, k4, k2tog, yo.
Row 47: K1 tbl, k3, k2tog, yo, k1.
Row 48: K1 tbl, k2, k2tog, yo, p1, k1 tbl.
Row 49: K1 tbl, k1, k2tog, yo, k1, p1, k1 tbl.
Row 50: K1 tbl, k2tog, yo, [p1, k1 tbl] 2 times.
Row 51: K2tog, yo, k1, [p1, k1 tbl] 2 times.
Rows 52-54: [K1 tbl, p1] 3 times, k1 tbl.

Round 1: *P1 (2), work from chart row 17 over 7 sts; repeat from * 3 more times, p1 (2), ssk, k to 2 sts before end of round, k2tog. 82 (88) sts.
Round 2: *P1 (2), work from chart row 18 over 7 sts; repeat from * 3 more times, p1 (2), k to end of round.
Last 2 rounds set chart pattern on instep and gusset decreases. Repeat these 2 rounds 9 (7) more times, working next row of chart each time. 64 (74) sts.

You should now have 33 (38) sts on instep and 31 (36) sts on sole.

FOOT

Work as set (chart pattern on instep and st st on sole) without further shaping until sock measures 5cm [2in] less than the desired foot length.

TOE

Round 1: K1, ssk, k27 (32), k2tog, k1, pm, k to end. 62 (72) sts.
Round 2: Knit.
Round 3: K1, ssk, k to 3 sts before marker, k2tog, k1, slm; repeat from * once more. 58 (68) sts.

Repeat last 2 rounds 10 (11) more times. 18 (24) sts.
Cut yarn, leaving a 30cm [12in] tail.
Graft sts together using Kitchener stitch. Weave in ends.

SOCK TWO

CUFF
Work as Sock One.

LEG
Round 1: *P1 (2), reading from right to left, work from row 28 of chart over 7 sts; repeat from * to end.
Round 2: *P1 (2), reading from right to left, work from row 29 of chart over 7 sts; repeat from * to end.
Last 2 rounds set reverse st st and chart patterns. Work as set until chart row 54 is complete, then work chart rows 1-42.

HEEL FLAP AND HEEL TURN
Work as Sock One.

GUSSET

Set-up Round: Sl1, k18 (19), pick up and knit 16 sts along edge of heel flap (1 stitch in each slipped stitch along the edge of the flap), work across instep sts as foll: *P1 (2), work from chart row 43 over 7 sts; repeat from * 3 more times, p1 (2), pick up and knit 16 sts along edge of heel flap, k35 (36). Place marker for new start of round (at start of instep stitches). 84 (90) sts.

Round 1: *P1 (2), work from chart row 44 over 7 sts; repeat from * 3 more times, p1 (2), ssk, k to 2 sts before end of round, k2tog. 82 (88) sts.
Round 2: *P1 (2), work from chart row 45 over 7 sts; repeat from * 3 more times, p1 (2), k to end of round.
Last 2 rounds set chart pattern on instep and gusset decreases. Repeat these 2 rounds 9 (7) more times, working next row of chart each time. 64 (74) sts.

You should now have 33 (38) sts on instep and 31 (36) sts on sole.

FOOT AND TOE
Work as Sock One.

Bright and cheerful knee-high socks that start with a ribbed cuff, leading to bands of stranded colourwork in bold geometric patterns.

Brighton!

Brighton

YARN

Long version: Fyberspates Sheila's Sock (100% superwash merino; 365m per 100g skein)
Colour 1: Pebble Beach, 1 x 100g skein
Colour 2: Gold, 1 x 100g skein
Colour 3: Dark Blue, 1 x 100g skein

Short version: The Knitting Goddess Merino and Nylon Sock (75% superwash merino, 25% nylon; 212m per 50g skein)
Colour 1: Mid Blue, 1 x 50g skein
Colour 2: Turquoise, 1 x 50g skein
Colour 3: Silver, 2 x 50g skeins

NEEDLES

2.25mm [UK 13/US 1] 80cm [30in] circular needles or DPNs (or size needed to get gauge)
Tapestry needle
Stitch markers

TENSION

36 sts and 50 rows = 10cm [4in] over st st
36 sts and 40 rows = 10cm [4in] over colourwork pattern

SIZES

Small (Medium, Large)
To fit foot circumference: 20 (23, 25.5) cm [8 (9, 10) in]
Actual foot circumference of sock:
16.5 (20, 23.5) cm [6.5 (8, 9.25) in]

ABBREVIATIONS

See full list of abbreviations on page 66.

PATTERN NOTES

There are different charts for Sock One and Sock Two, so that the colourwork patterns mirror each other.
You may need to use different sized needles for the plain and colourwork stocking stitch in order to maintain the same stitch tension.
The pattern gives instructions for a long and a short version of these socks.

SOCK ONE – LONG VERSION

CUFF

Using colour 1, cast on 96 (108, 120) sts. Distribute sts over your needles as desired and join to work in the round, being careful not to twist. Place marker for start of round.

Round 1: *K2, p2; repeat from * to end. Last round sets rib pattern. Work this round 55 more times.

LEG

Round 1: Reading from right to left, work from row 1 of chart A, repeating 12-stitch motif 8 (9, 10) times in total.

Last round sets chart A pattern. Continue to work from chart as set, until row 21 is complete.

Round 22 (dec): Using colour 3 only, *k6 (7, 8), k2tog; repeat from * to end. 84 (96, 108) sts.

Round 23: Reading from right to left, work from row 1 of chart B, repeating 12-stitch motif 7 (8, 9) times in total.

Last round sets chart B pattern. Continue to work from chart as set, until row 24 is complete.

Round 47 (dec): Using colour 3 only, *k5 (6, 7), k2tog; repeat from * to end. 72 (84, 96) sts.

Round 48: Reading from right to left, work from row 1 of chart A, repeating 12-stitch motif 6 (7, 8) times in total.

Last round sets chart A pattern. Cont to work from chart as set, until row 21 is complete.

Round 69 (dec): Using colour 3 only, *k4 (5, 6), k2tog; repeat from * to end. 60 (72, 84) sts.

Rounds 70-93: Work all 24 rows from chart B, repeating 12-stitch motif 5 (6, 7) times in total.
Round 94: Using colour 3 only, knit.

Rounds 95-115: Work all 21 rows from chart A, repeating 12-stitch motif 5, (6, 7) times in total.

Using colour 3 only, knit 3 rounds.
**Colour 3 only will be used for the rest of the sock.

HEEL FLAP

Turn work so WS is facing. Heel flap will be worked back and forth on the next 31 (37, 43) sts, beginning with a WS row. Keep remaining 29 (35, 41) sts on needles for instep.

Row 1 (WS): Sl1 wyif, p30 (36, 42).
Row 2 (RS): *Sl1 wyib, k1; repeat from * until 1 st remains, k1.

Repeat these 2 rows 14 more times then work row 1 once more.

TURN HEEL

Row 1 (RS): Sl1 wyib, k17 (19, 23), ssk, k1, turn, leaving remaining 10 (14, 16) sts unworked.
Row 2: Sl1 wyif, p6 (4, 6), p2tog, p1, turn, leaving remaining 10 (14, 16) sts unworked.
Row 3: Sl1 wyib, k to 1 st before gap, ssk, k1, turn.
Row 4: Sl1 wyif, p to 1 st before gap, p2tog, p1, turn.
Repeat last 2 rows 4 (6, 7) more times. All heel sts have been worked. 19 (21, 25) heel sts remain.

GUSSET

Set-up Round: Sl1, k18 (20, 24), pick up and knit 16 sts along edge of heel flap (1 stitch in each slipped stitch along the edge of the flap),

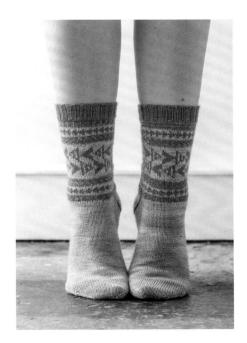

Charts

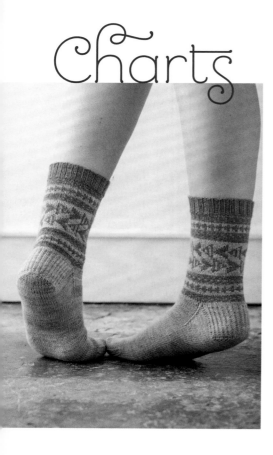

CHART D: SOCK TWO

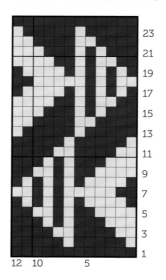

CHART B: SOCK ONE

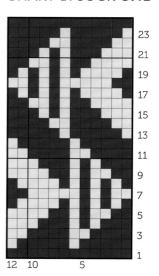

CHART C: SOCK TWO

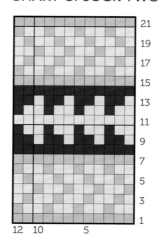

CHART A: SOCK ONE

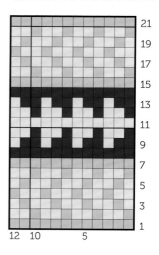

KEY

☐ Colour 1; Knit

☐ Colour 2; Knit

■ Colour 3; Knit

knit across 29 (35, 41) instep stitches, pick up and knit 16 sts along edge of heel flap, k35 (37, 41). Place marker for new start of round (at start of instep stitches). 80 (88, 98) sts.

Round 1: K30 (36, 42) across instep sts, ssk, k to 2 sts before end of round, k2tog. 78 (86, 96) sts.
Round 2: Knit.

Repeat these 2 rounds 10 (8, 7) more times. 58 (70, 82) sts.
You should now have 29 (35, 41) sts each on instep and sole.

FOOT
Knit all rounds, until the sock measures 5cm [2in] less than the desired foot length.

TOE
Round 1: Knit.
Round 2: K1, ssk, k23 (29, 35), k2tog, k1, pm, k1, ssk, k23 (29, 35), k2tog, k1. 56 (68, 80) sts.
Round 3: Knit.
Round 4: *K1, ssk, k to 3 sts before marker, k2tog, k1, slm; repeat from * once more. 52 (64, 76) sts.
Repeat last 2 rounds 8 (10, 13) more times. 20 (24, 24) sts.
Cut yarn, leaving a 30cm [12in] tail. Graft sts together using Kitchener stitch. Weave in ends.

SOCK TWO – LONG VERSION

CUFF AND LEG
Using chart C instead of chart A, and chart D instead of chart B, work as Sock One to **.

Partial round: Using colour 3 only, k30 (36, 42).

HEEL, FOOT AND TOE
Work as for Sock One to end.

SOCK ONE – SHORT VERSION

CUFF
Using colour 1, cast on 60 (72, 84) sts. Distribute sts over your needles as desired and join to work in the round, being careful not to twist. Place marker for start of round.

Round 1: *K2, p2; repeat from * to end. Last round sets rib pattern. Work this round 15 more times.

LEG
Round 1: Reading from right to left, work from row 1 of chart A, repeating 12-stitch motif 5 (6, 7) times in total.

Last round sets chart A pattern. Continue to work from chart as set, until row 21 is complete.

Round 22: Using colour 3 only, knit.
Round 23: Reading from right to left, work from row 1 of chart B, repeating 12-stitch motif 5 (6, 7) times in total.

Last round sets chart B pattern. Continue to work from chart as set, until row 24 is complete.

Round 47: Using colour 3 only, knit.
Rounds 48-68: Work all 21 rows of chart A again.

Using colour 3 only, knit 3 rounds.
**Colour 3 only will be used for the rest of the sock.

HEEL, FOOT AND TOE
Work as for Sock One, Long Version, to end.

SOCK TWO – SHORT VERSION

CUFF AND LEG
Using chart C instead of chart A, and chart D instead of chart B, work as Sock One to **.

Partial round: Using colour 3 only, k30 (36, 42).

HEEL, FOOT AND TOE
Work as for Sock One, Long Version, to end.

Intricate cables, texture and twisted stitches form lines of pattern, echoing vintage patchwork quilting.

Saxifrage

Saxifrage

YARN
Opal 4-ply (75% superwash wool, 25% polyamide; 425m per 100g ball)
Violet (3072), 1 x 100g ball

NEEDLES
2.25mm [UK 13/US 1] 80cm [30in] circular needles or DPNs (or size needed to get gauge)
Cable needle
Tapestry needle
Stitch markers

TENSION
36 sts and 50 rows = 10cm [4in] over st st
37.5 sts and 50 rows = 10cm [4in] over unstretched twisted st cable panels

SIZES
Small (Large)
To fit foot circumference: 20 (25.5) cm [8 (10) in]
Actual foot circumference of sock, unstretched: 18.5 (21) cm [7.25 (8.25) in]

ABBREVIATIONS
1/1 LPT: Slip next st to cable needle and place at front of work, p1, then k1 tbl from cable needle
1/1 RPT: Slip next st to cable needle and place at back of work, k1 tbl, then p1 from cable needle
1/1 LT: Slip next st to cable needle and place at front of work, k1 tbl, then k1 tbl from cable needle
1/1 RT: Slip next st to cable needle and place at back of work, k1 tbl, then k1 tbl from cable needle
2/1 RPT: Slip next st to cable needle and place at back of work, k2 tbl, then p1 from cable needle
2/1 LPT: Slip next 2 sts to cable needle and place at front of work, p1, then k2 tbl from cable needle
2/1 RT: Slip next st to cable needle and place at back of work, k2 tbl, then k1 tbl from cable needle
2/1 LT: Slip next 2 sts to cable needle and place at front of work, k1 tbl, then k2 tbl from cable needle
3 st loop: Insert right needle into third st on left needle and draw this st over first 2 sts on left needle; k1, yo, k1

See full list of abbreviations on page 66.

PATTERN NOTES

There are different charts for Sock One and Sock Two, as the cables mirror each other.

SOCK ONE

CUFF

Cast on 69 (78) sts. Distribute sts over your needles as desired and join to work in the round, being careful not to twist. Place marker for start of round.

Round 1: Reading from right to left, work from row 1 of chart A (B) and repeat the 23 (26)-stitch motif 3 times in total.
Repeat last round 11 more times to create twisted rib pattern.

Round 13: Reading from right to left, work from row 2 of chart A (B) and repeat the 23 (26)-stitch motif 3 times in total.
Last round sets chart A (B) pattern.

Continue to work as set until row 6 of chart A (B) is complete.

LEG

Round 1: *P1 (2), work 9 sts from row 1 of chart C, p1 (2), work 4 sts from row 1 of chart D, p1 (2), work 9 sts from row 1 of chart E; repeat from * 2 more times.
Round 2: *P1 (2), work 9 sts from row 2 of chart C, p1 (2), work 4 sts from row 2 of chart D, p1 (2), work 7 sts from row 2 of chart E; repeat from * 2 more times.
Last 2 rounds set chart patterns and reverse stocking stitch. Cont to work as set until row 32 of the charts has been completed for the second time.

HEEL FLAP

Turn work so WS is facing. Heel flap will be worked back and forth on the next 35 (39) sts, beginning with a WS row. Keep remaining 34 (39) sts on needles for instep.

Row 1 (WS): Sl1 wyif, p34 (38).
Row 2 (RS): *Sl1 wyib, k1; repeat from * until 1 st remains, k1.

Repeat these 2 rows 14 more times then work row 1 once more.

TURN HEEL

Row 1 (RS): Sl1 wyib, k19 (21), ssk, k1, turn, leaving remaining 12 (14) sts unworked.
Row 2: Sl1 wyif, p6, p2tog, p1, turn, leaving remaining 12 (14) sts unworked.
Row 3: Sl1 wyib, k to 1 st before gap, ssk, k1, turn.
Row 4: Sl1 wyif, p to 1 st before gap, p2tog, p1, turn.
Repeat last 2 rows 5 (6) more times. All heel sts have been worked. 21 (23) heel sts remain.

GUSSET

Set-up Round: Sl1, k20 (22), pick up and knit 16 sts along edge of heel flap (1 stitch in each slipped stitch along the edge of the flap), work across instep sts as foll: p1 (2), work 9 sts from row 1 of chart C, p1 (2), work 4 sts from row 1 of chart D, p1 (2), work 7 sts from row 1 of chart E, p1 (2), work 9 sts from row 1 of chart C, p1 (2), pick up and knit 16 sts along edge of heel flap, k37 (39). Place marker for new start of round (at start of instep stitches). 87 (94) sts.

Round 1: P1 (2), work 9 sts from row 2 of chart C, p1 (2), work 4 sts from row 2 of chart D, p1 (2), work 7 sts from row 2 of chart E, p1 (2), work 9 sts from row 2 of chart C, p1 (2), ssk, k to 2 sts before end of round, k2tog. 85 (92) sts.
Round 2: P1 (2), work 9 sts from row 3 of chart C, p1 (2), work 4 sts from row 3 of chart D, p1 (2), work 7 sts from row 3 of chart E, p1 (2), work 9 sts from row 3 of chart C, p1 (2), k to end of round.

Charts

CHART H:
LARGE CABLE RIGHT

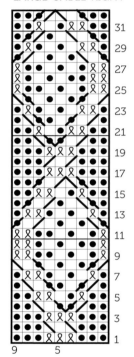

CHART E:
LOOP ST PANEL

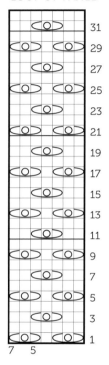

CHART D:
SMALL CABLE

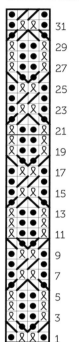

CHART C:
LARGE CABLE LEFT

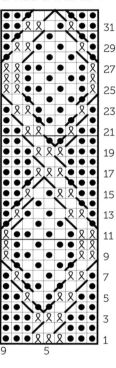

KEY

☐	Knit
●	Purl
⅄	K1 tbl
⟍	1/1 LPT
⟋	1/1 RPT
⟍	1/1 LT
⟋	1/1 RT
⟋	2/1 RPT
⟍	2/1 LPT
⟋	2/1 RT
⟍	2/1 LT
⊂O⊃	3 st loop
☐	Pattern repeat

CHART G: SOCK TWO CUFF, LARGE

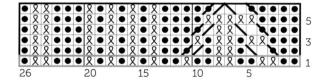

CHART F: SOCK TWO CUFF, SMALL

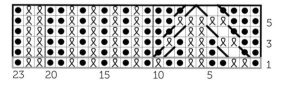

CHART B: SOCK ONE CUFF, LARGE

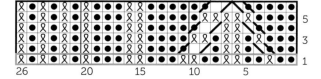

CHART A: SOCK ONE CUFF, SMALL

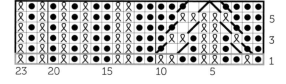

Last 2 rounds set chart patterns and gusset decreases. Repeat these 2 rounds 8 (7) more times, working next row of charts each time. 69 (78) sts.

Small only
Next round: Work in pattern across instep stitches, ssk, k to end. 68 sts.

All sizes
68 (78) sts remain: 34 (39) sts each on instep and sole.

FOOT
Work as set (with charts and reverse stocking stitch on instep, and stocking stitch on sole) without further shaping in pattern as set until sock measures 5cm [2in] less than the desired foot length.

TOE
Round 1: Knit.
Round 2: K1, ssk, k28 (33), k2tog, k1, pm, k1, ssk, k28 (33), k2tog, k1. 64 (74) sts.
Round 3: Knit.
Round 4: *K1, ssk, k to 3 sts before marker, k2tog, k1, slm; repeat from * once more. 60 (70) sts.
Repeat last 2 rounds 10 (12) more times. 20 (22) sts.
Cut yarn, leaving a 30cm [12in] tail. Graft sts together using Kitchener stitch. Weave in ends.

SOCK TWO

CUFF
Cast on 69 (78) sts. Distribute sts over your needles as desired and join to work in the round, being careful not to twist. Place marker for start of round.

Round 1: Reading from right to left, work from row 1 of chart F (G) and repeat the 23 (26)-stitch motif 3 times in total. Complete Sock Two cuff as for Sock One cuff, working from chart F (G) instead of chart A (B).

LEG
Round 1: *P1 (2), work 9 sts from row 1 of chart H, p1 (2), work 7 sts from row 1 of chart E, p1 (2), work 4 sts from row 1 of chart D; repeat from * 2 more times.
Round 2: *P1 (2), work 9 sts from row 2 of chart H, p1 (2), work 7 sts from row 2 of chart E, p1 (2), work 4 sts from row 2 of chart D; repeat from * 2 more times.
Last 2 rounds set chart patterns and reverse stocking stitch. Cont to work as set until row 32 of the charts has been completed for the second time.

HEEL FLAP AND HEEL TURN
Work as for Sock One.

GUSSET
Set-up Round: Sl1, k20 (22), pick up and knit 16 sts along edge of heel flap (1 stitch in each slipped stitch along the edge of the flap), work across instep sts as foll: p1 (2), work 9 sts from row 1 of chart H, p1 (2), work 7 sts from row 1 of chart E, p1 (2), work 4 sts from row 1 of chart D, p1 (2), work 9 sts from row 1 of chart H, p1 (2), pick up and knit 16 sts along edge of heel flap, k37 (39).

Place marker for new start of round (at start of instep stitches). 87 (94) sts.

Round 1: P1 (2), work 9 sts from row 2 of chart H, p1 (2), work 7 sts from row 2 of chart E, p1 (2), work 4 sts from row 2 of chart D, p1 (2), work 9 sts from row 2 of chart H, p1 (2), ssk, k to 2 sts before end of round, k2tog. 85 (92) sts.
Round 2: P1 (2), work 9 sts from row 3 of chart H, p1 (2), work 7 sts from row 3 of chart E, p1 (2), work 4 sts from row 3 of chart D, p1 (2), work 9 sts from row 3 of chart H, p1 (2), k to end of round.
Complete gusset as for Left Sock, working from charts as set by last 2 rounds.

FOOT AND TOE
Work as for Sock One.

Abbreviations

cm	Centimetres
cont	Continue
dec(s)	Decrease(s)/decreasing
DPN(s)	Double-pointed needle(s)
foll(s)	Follow(s)/following
g	Grams
in	Inches
k	Knit
k2tog	Knit the next two stitches together
m	Metres
mm	Millimetres
p	Purl
p2tog	Purl two stitches together
pm	Place marker
RS	Right side
sl1	Slip one stitch
slm	Slip marker
ssk	Slip two stitches knitwise one at a time, knit two slipped stitches together through back of loop
st st	Stocking stitch (US: Stockinette stitch)
st(s)	Stitch(es)
tbl	Through the back loop
wrap 3	K3 onto cable needle, wrap yarn twice around these stitches by bringing yarn to front of work between the left needle and the cable needle and wrapping yarn to back of work between cable needle and right needle, then slip the 3 stitches from the cable needle to the right needle.
WS	Wrong side
wyib	With yarn in back
wyif	With yarn in front
yo	Yarnover
1/1 LPC	Slip next st to cable needle and place at front of work, p1, then k1 from cable needle
1/1 RPC	Slip next st to cable needle and place at back of work, k1, then p1 from cable needle
1/1 LPT	Slip next st to cable needle and place at front of work, p1, then k1 tbl from cable needle
1/1 RPT	Slip next st to cable needle and place at back of work, k1 tbl, then p1 from cable needle
1/1 LT	Slip next st to cable needle and place at front of work, k1 tbl, then k1 tbl from cable needle
1/1 RT	Slip next st to cable needle and place at back of work, k1 tbl, then k1 tbl from cable needle
2/1 RC	Slip next st to cable needle and place at back of work, k2, then k1 from cable needle
2/1 LC	Slip next 2 sts to cable needle and place at front of work, k1, then k2 from cable needle
2/1 RPC	Slip next st to cable needle and place at back of work, k2, then p1 from cable needle
2/1 LPC	Slip next 2 sts to cable needle and place at front of work, p1, then k2 from cable needle
2/1 RPT	Slip next st to cable needle and place at back of work, k2 tbl, then p1 from cable needle
2/1 LPT	Slip next 2 sts to cable needle and place at front of work, p1, then k2 tbl from cable needle
2/1 RT	Slip next st to cable needle and place at back of work, k2 tbl, then k1 tbl from cable needle
2/1 LT	Slip next 2 sts to cable needle and place at front of work, k1 tbl, then k2 tbl from cable needle
2/1/2 RPC	Slip next 3 sts to cable needle and place at back of work, k2, slip left-most st from cable needle back on to LH needle, move cable needle with remaining sts to front of work, p1 from LH needle, then k2 from cable needle.
2/1/2 LPC	Slip next 3 sts to cable needle and place at front of work, k2, move left-most st from cable needle back on to LH needle, p this st, then k2 from cable needle.
2/2 RC	Slip next 2 sts to cable needle and place at back of work, k2, then k2 from cable needle
2/2 LC	Slip next 2 sts to cable needle and place at front of work, k2, then k2 from cable needle
2/2 RPC	Slip next 2 sts to cable needle and place at back of work, k2, then p2 from cable needle
2/2 LPC	Slip next sts to cable needle and place at front of work, p2, then k2 from cable needle
3 st loop	Insert right needle into third st on left needle and draw this st over first 2 sts on left needle; k1, yo, k1

How to...

AFTERTHOUGHT HEEL

This type of heel is used in the Paignton cabled sock pattern on page 42.

1. Return to the line of waste yarn that was knitted as part of the heel set-up instructions.

2. With RS facing, pick up the right leg of each stitch directly below the row of waste yarn. Use two DPNs, picking up half the total number of stitches on each needle.

3. Turn the sock and repeat Step 2, picking up the stitches on the other side of the waste yarn.

4. The stitches above and below the waste yarn are now spread across four DPNs. If using circular needles, pick up first side on needle tip, slide the stitches onto the cable, and pick up the second side on the needle tip.

5. Carefully remove the waste yarn, taking care that no stitches were missed from the picking up process.

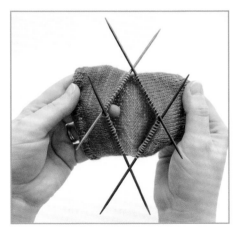

6. The live stitches are now spread across four DPNs and are ready to work.

KITCHENER STITCH (GRAFTING)

Every sock in this book uses Kitchener stitch to close the toe stitches. This tutorial shows you how, and gives tips on making the graft stitches neat and tidy.

1. Holding needles parallel to each other, thread a tapestry needle with the yarn tail. Insert the tapestry needle into the first stitch on the DPN closest to you **as if to purl** and pull it through, leaving the stitch **on** the needle.

2. Insert the needle into the first stitch on the DPN furthest from you **as if to knit** and pull it through, leaving the stitch **on** the needle.

3. Insert the needle into the first stitch on the DPN closest to you **as if to knit** and pull it through, slipping the stitch **off** the needle.

4. Insert the needle into the first stitch on the DPN closest to you **as if to purl** and pull it through, leaving the stitch **on** the needle.

5. Insert the needle into the first stitch on the DPN furthest from you **as if to purl** and pull it through, slipping the stitch **off** the needle.

6. Insert the needle into the first stitch on the DPN furthest from you **as if to knit** and pull it through, leaving the stitch **on** the needle.

FINISHING

Repeat steps 3-6 until all the live stitches have been grafted together.
The grafted stitches will be looser than the knitted stitches around them. Use the tapestry needle to neaten them: starting at the first stitch to be grafted, pull each stitch until it matches the knitted stitches on the toe. Take the yarn to the inside of the sock and weave in the end to finish.

LONG-TAIL CAST-ON

This cast-on method gives a firm but flexible edge that is perfect for socks.

1. Measure approximately 1m [1yd] of yarn, place the yarn over the needle with the ball at the rear and the tail of the yarn towards you. Use your forefinger to hold the yarn on the needle.

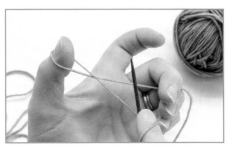

2. Using the tail end of the yarn, make a loop of yarn around your thumb as shown.

3. Put the needle tip into the loop.

4. Use your right hand to wrap the yarn from the ball side around the needle tip.

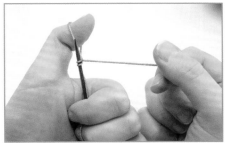

5. Use your thumb to lift the loop off the end of the needle, thus making the first (formed by holding the yarn over the needle) and second stitches.

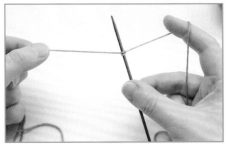

6. Gently tighten both ends of the yarn (tail and ball sides).

CONTINUE AS SET
Repeat steps 2 to 6 until you have cast on the desired number of stitches.

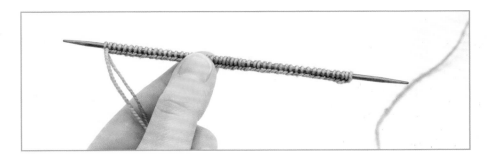

Why knit socks?

You will often be asked why you would bother to knit socks when you could just buy a pair very easily for not very much money.

Here's my take...

» Socks are a small and portable making them perfect commuting or travel companions.
» Many knitters will have a sock project on the go as well as a larger garment, so that they have something to take along on trips outside the house.
» Hand-knitted socks are warmer and more comfortable than most shop-bought socks.
» Socks are also a good way to learn new techniques, small and much quicker to get to the "finished object" stage than a garment.
» They are possibly the ideal use for the beautifully unique hand-dyed yarns that are available around the world.
» Most socks can be knitted from 100g of yarn or less.

I'm sure there are many (many) more reasons to knit socks – of course, the perfect answer to this question is always...

"Because I can!"

The following pages have some good tips to get the best results from your sock knitting adventures.

TOP TIPS FOR SOCK KNITTERS

Here are some of my top tips for knitting socks:

WORK AT A TIGHT TENSION

Make sure that your knitted fabric is firm. Working at a tight tension ensures that your socks will last longer and won't sag. When stitches in fabric are too large, the yarn moves around more and rubs against itself, which causes wear. I usually work at a stocking stitch tension of 36 sts and 50 rows to 10cm [4in], which gives a firm, hard-wearing fabric in most standard sock yarns.

CHOOSING YARNS – COLOURS

Most of my textured sock designs will require a solid or semi-solid coloured yarn. Too much variegation in the colours makes the texture patterns hard to see. When choosing yarns for colourwork socks, such as Brighton, be sure to check that all shades are colourfast before casting on. You can do this by soaking a portion of your skein in tepid water and then pressing the damp yarn on some kitchen roll. If any colour comes off on the towel it may require further rinsing before you knit with it. If colour continues to bleed, contact your hand-dyer for further advice.

CHOOSING YARNS – FIBRES

Some sock yarns have a nylon content, this can help strengthen the socks and make them last longer. A sock yarn which is 100% wool and has no nylon can also wear well, so long as it is knitted at a firm tension. Sock yarns with a small amount of silk can also be very strong. Yarns that are specifically intended for socks are often spun tightly and made from blends that are well-suited to knitting socks.

CASTING ON

I recommend using the Long-Tail Cast-On Method when casting on for socks. This gives a firm, but stretchy edge to your cuff. You will find a step-by-step tutorial on page 69. There is also a link to an online video tutorial shown on the next page.

TENSION

Obtaining the correct tension (US: gauge) for both the stocking stitch and stitch patterns in your sock is vital to creating a sock that fits. The needle sizes given are suggestions. Every knitter is different, and the fact that your tension matches in stocking stitch does not guarantee that it will match in the pattern stitch. It may not seem worth knitting a separate swatch in the round, but please be sure to check that you are getting the correct tension once you have knitted 10cm [4in] of the main leg pattern. This will save you from having to rip out a whole sock later.

Once you have knitted 10cm [4in] of the main leg pattern, carefully measure the number of stitches and rows over the central 10cm [4in]. If you have the correct number of stitches and rows, you are using the correct sized needles. If you have too many stitches (and rows), you will need to start again with larger needles. If you have too few stitches (and rows), you will need to try smaller needles.

It is very important to match the tension given in *both* stitch patterns; the needle size that you use to do this does not matter. It is the tension that determines the finished size of your socks and how much yarn is used.

SOCK SIZING

The socks in this book are all designed with negative ease. This means that the socks have a smaller foot circumference than your feet do. All of the stitch patterns used are inherently stretchy, so to ensure that your socks don't sag, they need to be knitted a little smaller than your foot size.

You will notice that no foot lengths are given in the patterns. This is because all socks can be knitted to the exact foot length required. Very long foot lengths may require more yarn; all of the samples were knitted to a foot length of 23cm [9in]. If you don't know the foot length of your sock recipient, the following sizing table may prove useful:

UK shoe size	2	2.5	3	3.5	4	4.5	5	5.5	6	6.5	7	7.5	8
US shoe size	4.5	5	5.5	6	6.5	7	7.5	8	8.5	9	9.5	10	10.5
Foot length (cm)	21.5	22	22.5	23	23	23.5	24	24	24.5	25	25.5	26	26.5

Where there is only one set of numbers in a pattern instruction, it refers to all sizes. When more than one number is given, the smallest size appears first, with the larger sizes appearing inside brackets in size order. It is always useful to circle or highlight the size you are working throughout the pattern before you start. Read the pattern carefully, as sometimes smaller groups of sizes are treated separately. It is always marked clearly where the instructions return to all sizes.

USING CHARTS

Charts are a graphical representation of your knitting, with each square representing a stitch (or small group of stitches) and every row of squares representing a round of knitting. All chart rows are read from right to left, since the sock designs in this book are all knitted in the round.

We have given written instructions for the charts of as many of the patterns as possible – in some cases the written instructions would be prohibitively long.

This article from Knitty.com is a helpful tutorial on knitting from charts: **www.tinyurl.com/KnittingCharts**

REPEATING INSTRUCTIONS

Where a pattern tells you to repeat from * a certain number more times, it means that you should work the instruction once, and then work it a further number of times as instructed. For example, *p1, k1 tbl; repeat from * 2 more times. This means that you repeat "p1, k1 tbl" three times in total (p1, k1 tbl, p1, k1 tbl, p1, k1 tbl).

SQUARE BRACKETS

Some patterns have instructions given within square brackets. After the bracket it will tell you how many times to work that instruction in total. For example, [k3, p1 tbl] 3 times. This would be worked as k3, p1 tbl, k3, p1 tbl, k3, p1 tbl.

TECHNIQUES REFERENCE SOURCES
BOOKS
A good general knitting techniques book will be invaluable for helping you with some of the methods used in this book. We recommend **The Knitting Answer Book** by Margaret Radcliffe. ISBN 978-0715325759

Words of wisdom

ONLINE TUTORIALS
The internet is a great source of helpful tutorials and techniques videos. Here are some handy resources:

Knitting in the round is well-described in videos at KnittingHelp.com, which cover how to use double-pointed needles, two circular needles and the Magic Loop method **www.tinyurl.com/KnittingInTheRound**

The **long-tail cast-on method** shown on page 67 is shown in a video here: http://verypink.com/2010/03/13/video-long-tail-cast-on/

An **alternative long-tail cast-on** style is shown in a video at KnittingHelp.com: **www.tinyurl.com/CastOnMethods**

Kitchener stitch (grafting) (shown on page 68) is also covered in this article from Knitty.com: **www.tinyurl.com/KitchenerStitch**

CARE INSTRUCTIONS
Take care to follow the washing instructions on your ball band. Many sock yarns are machine washable at 40C on a gentle cycle. Generally, hand-dyed yarns will keep their colours longer if they are hand-washed.

PATTERN QUERIES
If you think there may be an error with any of the pattern instructions, please email **coopknit@gmail.com**

KEEP IN TOUCH
My blog and online shop are at **www.coopknits.co.uk**

The Coop Knits group on Ravelry is friendly and funny. Please do join the group and share pictures of your finished Coop Knits projects, or tell me about what you're working on now. I love to see what you have been making.
www.ravelry.com/groups/coop-knits

You can find me on Twitter at **@CoopKnits** – don't forget to follow me, to keep up-to-date with new pattern releases.

And finally...

To Nic, Jen, my husband, Jesse, Jeni, Caroline, Ashley, Pepita, Joy, Mandy and Paula - thank you all for your help with this book.